wok it

wok it

recipes + techniques + cooking tips

MURDOCH BOOKS

contents

wok basics

Invented centuries ago, woks remain the quintessential way to cook Asian food. And, as the popularity of Asian cuisine has increased worldwide, the wok has moved far beyond its traditional home to kitchens around the world. Woks work on the principle of bringing food very close to the heat source. The basic design has remained unchanged for centuries as both the shape and material of woks allow them to evenly absorb heat, and to retain and transmit it quickly across the entire surface area. Wok cooking offers a quick, healthy way of cooking. The wok's wide surface area means that little oil needs to be used to cook food. Also, the fast cooking of stir-fries and many steamed dishes, in particular, retains the nutrient values of the ingredients to a larger extent than many other cooking methods.

what sort of wok should I buy?

While all woks are based on the same fundamental design there are some variations. Size, for instance. For general domestic cooking, a 30–35 cm (12–14 inch) diameter wok is the most versatile size, as it is easier to cook small batches of food in a large wok than vice versa.

Some woks have two handles on either side and some have only one long handle. Two-handled woks are more stable, which is valuable when steaming or deep-frying, whereas one-handled woks are better for stir-frying, as the handle can be held in one hand and the charn (a spade-like scoop) in the other to create the constant movement required when stir-frying.

Woks are available with either a round or flat bottom. Round-bottomed woks are best suited to cooking on a gas stove, as the flames can be regulated to reach up and hit the exterior of the wok. A wok stand can be used to ensure that the wok remains stable on the stove. Flat-bottomed woks are a better option if cooking on an electric stove, as this ensures the surface is in constant contact with the heat source.

choosing the right material

Originally, woks were made from cast iron, and some cooks still prefer to use these, as cast iron retains heat well. But as cast-iron woks are very heavy they are not suitable for everyone. Today, you can choose from many other materials. The most common material in Asian countries is lightweight carbon steel. A good heat conductor, it promotes good searing and flavour, especially when used on a gas stove.

Stainless steel is another popular choice; however, it is not a good heat conductor unless sandwiched between another metal that conducts heat well, such as aluminium. With the growth of more health-conscious cooking, non-stick woks have also become popular. They are easy to clean and require minimal oil. However, many manufacturers of non-stick products advise against using them over high heat, and high heat is essential for successful stir-frying. There are newer anodized non-stick woks on the market that may be able to withstand high temperatures, but check with the manufacturer.

Another option is the electric wok, but once again getting the high heat needed for successful stir-frying is not always possible, so make sure you choose the highest wattage possible.

All woks, except non-stick ones, must be cleaned and seasoned before use (see page 14 for a step-by-step guide). This is to remove the coating that is placed on these woks to stop them rusting before being bought. Once you've seasoned your wok, repeat the oiling process just prior to cooking with your wok for the first time. With continued use over time, a coating builds up and provides a non-stick effect. In fact, carbon steel woks turn a brownish-black colour through continued use, which is not only normal, but is also highly desirable. This filmy layer of residue cooks onto the wok with the high heat and imparts the distinctive and somewhat smoky wok aroma. For many, this defines an authentic stir-fry.

looking after your wok

Cast-iron, stainless steel or non-stick woks should be treated as you would any other utensils made from these materials. To clean a carbon steel wok, first allow it to cool, then wash it with hot water, using a soft brush or cloth. Avoid using detergents unless absolutely necessary, as they damage the seasoning. Ensure that the wok is dried thoroughly before storing. You may want to sit it over low heat for 1–2 minutes to make sure it is completely dry. To keep carbon steel woks in top condition, they should be wiped or brushed inside with a thin layer of oil before being stored.

A properly seasoned carbon steel wok should rarely, if ever, be scoured with an abrasive material like steel wool. The outside, however, may occasionally need to be scrubbed. If you do burn something in the wok, you may need to use detergent and even a piece of fine steel wool to clean your wok. It will then need re-seasoning.

charn

Essential if you do a lot of stir-frying.

A charn or wok turner is a spade-like

scoop that is ideal for the continuous

fast scooping and turning required

when stir-frying.

steamer

Bamboo steamers are useful for cooking a wide range of foods, from dumplings to whole fish, and can go straight from the wok to the table.

spider

This is a circular steel-mesh strainer often attached to a long bamboo handle. Useful for lifting and draining deep-fried food without bringing too much oil with the food. They are available in many different sizes.

wok stand

An important safety device to keep the wok steady on the stovetop. Use when deep-frying, steaming and cooking one-pots.

seasoning your wok

Using a scourer, **scrub off** the coating with detergent and hot water. Dry the wok.

To season the wok, put it over low heat. Add 2 tablespoons of vegetable oil and **rub over** the entire inner surface using paper towels.

Heat the wok slowly for 10–15 minutes, then wipe again with kitchen paper. The paper will blacken.

Repeat this process until the paper **wipes clean**. With continuous use, the wok will blacken entirely and develop a non-stick coating.

15

stir-frying

what is stir-frying?

Stir-frying is the classic wok cooking experience and is arguably the most fun to prepare. It involves the quick cooking of small pieces of food over high heat.

Stir-frying is regarded as a healthy cooking method as the rapid cooking time preserves many of the food's nutrients, particularly in vegetables, as well as its flavour, colour and texture. In addition, properly seasoned woks need very little oil as they develop a non-stick coating, and the oil that is used does not have time to be absorbed by the rapidly moving food. The wide, conical shape of the wok continually tips food back into the centre where the heat is at its most intense, thus searing food, cooking it in a few minutes and imparting a delicious smoky flavour.

getting ready to stir-fry

Remember that once you begin, you must keep going. There is no time to interrupt cooking to chop an ingredient or mix together a sauce. All ingredients should be prepared before you even heat the wok. This prevents food already in the wok from burning and ensures the quick and even cooking of all ingredients.

Choosing the right oil is important to both the method and flavour of stir-fries. The oil should have a high burning point due to the intensity of the heat required for successful stir-frying. It should also complement but not interfere with the main flavours. Suitable oils include peanut, sunflower, canola and vegetable oil. Avoid olive oil as it has a much stronger flavour.

Cut vegetables into small, even pieces, so that they cook rapidly and evenly. Long vegetables, such as leafy vegetable stems, asparagus and green beans should be cut on the diagonal, to increase their exposed surface area and hasten the cooking time. Washed vegetables should be dried thoroughly so that they don't stew.

Meat or poultry fillets should be sliced into thin, uniform-sized slices across the grain. This helps to tenderize the meat by breaking up the fibres, allowing the meat to cook quickly and evenly so that it retains its juices and remains tender rather than becoming tough.

If you're making a stir-fry sauce, combine the ingredients in advance — you won't have time when you're in the middle of stir-frying.

stir-frying — the event

Even before any oil is added, heat your wok over high heat. This enables the oil to be swirled around to coat the wok's entire surface before it has a chance to burn and taint the flavour of the food. If the recipe uses ginger or garlic it will usually be added straight after the oil, before the oil starts to smoke, as both ingredients can burn very quickly.

Add ingredients that take the longest to cook first, leaving fast-cooking food, such as leafy green vegetables, bean sprouts or snowpeas (mangetout) until last. If you are cooking meat, it may be the first ingredient introduced to the wok. Always add it in batches, adding just enough to form a single layer. Leave it to cook briefly before starting to toss from the centre of the wok to the sides, so that it seals and doesn't stick to the bottom of the wok and tear when turned. Never be tempted to add too much meat (or seafood for that matter) at a time as it will simply stew in its juices. Frequently, once the meat has been cooked, it is set aside while the other ingredients are cooked. The meat is then returned to the wok to be heated through and combined with the other ingredients, usually at the same time that any seasoning ingredients are added.

If you are cooking meat that has been marinated, make sure that you drain the meat thoroughly before cooking. It might be tempting to add the marinade for flavour, but if you add it too early, all you are doing is encouraging the meat to stew in its juices.

Usually vegetables and noodles are added once the meat has been cooked, and tossed constantly from the centre of the wok to the sides.

Additional flavourings are added towards the end of cooking to unify the dish and bring all the flavours together. Another reason for adding strong flavourings towards the end of the cooking time is because if salty seasonings, such as soy sauce, were added earlier, the salt can draw out the liquid of other ingredients and make them go soggy.

For saucy dishes, the method can be slightly different. The sauce ingredients are added to the wok first and then reduced to a glossy consistency before returning the meat or other vegetables to the wok to coat with sauce.

and finally

Always maintain the heat of your wok. You may need to reheat the wok between batches, to ensure that the heat is intense enough to sear the food, seal in any juices and prevent stewing. Remember, the temperature will drop once the food is added.

stir-frying techniques

Chop vegetables into small, bite-sized pieces.

When the wok is hot, add the oil and **swirl to coat** the base and sides.

Cook slices of meat in a **single layer** to prevent them stewing.

Add seasoning ingredients such as soy or fish sauce **at the end** of cooking.

caramel prawns

serves 4

1 tablespoon **peanut oil**

24 **raw king prawns (shrimp)**, peeled and deveined, tails intact

2 **garlic cloves**, crushed

3 **red Asian shallots**, finely chopped

60 g (2¼ oz/⅓ cup) grated **palm sugar**

2 tablespoons **fish sauce**

2 tablespoons **rice vinegar**

2 tablespoons chopped **coriander (cilantro) leaves**

lime wedges, to serve (optional)

Heat a wok over high heat, add the oil and swirl to coat. Add the prawns, garlic and shallots and stir-fry for about 1 minute, or until the prawns just start turning pink. Remove and set aside.

Put the sugar, fish sauce and vinegar in the wok with 125 ml (4 fl oz/½ cup) of water and boil for 5–10 minutes, or until reduced and syrupy. Return the prawns to the wok and stir-fry for 1–2 minutes, or until they are cooked through and coated with the caramel sauce. Stir in the coriander and serve with lime wedges, if desired.

sichuan chicken stir-fry

serves 4

500 g (1 lb 2 oz) **chicken tenderloins,**
  cut into thin strips

1/4 teaspoon **five-spice powder**

1 tablespoon **Chinese rice wine**

1 tablespoon **light soy sauce**

1 tablespoon **chilli bean paste**
  (toban djan)

2 teaspoons **Chinese black vinegar**

2 teaspoons **dark soy sauce**

3 tablespoons **chicken stock**

3 tablespoons **peanut oil**

1 small **red onion,** halved and thinly
  sliced lengthways (not into rings)

2 **garlic cloves,** crushed

2 teaspoons finely grated fresh **ginger**

1/2 teaspoon **Sichuan peppercorns,**
  crushed

4 **long dried red chillies,** cut in half
  lengthways

Put the chicken in a non-metallic bowl and sprinkle the five-spice powder over the top. Add the rice wine and light soy sauce, turn the chicken until well coated, then cover and marinate in the refrigerator for 1 hour.

Combine the chilli bean paste, vinegar, dark soy sauce and stock in a small jug.

Heat a wok until very hot, add 1 tablespoon of the oil and swirl to coat. Stir-fry the chicken in batches for 3 minutes, or until browned. Remove each batch and keep warm. Add another tablespoon of the oil, stir-fry the onion for 2 minutes, then remove and set aside with the chicken. Heat the remaining oil in the wok, add the garlic, ginger and peppercorns and stir-fry for 30 seconds, or until fragrant. Add the chilli and stir-fry for 15 seconds, or until it starts to change colour and darken.

Return the chicken and onion to the wok, add the sauce and toss for 3 minutes, or until completely cooked through and the sauce has thickened to coat the chicken. Serve immediately with rice.

singapore pepper crab

serves 4

1 tablespoon **dark soy sauce**

1 tablespoon **light soy sauce**

2 tablespoons **oyster sauce**

1 tablespoon **soft brown sugar**

8 raw **blue swimmer crabs**

1–2 tablespoons **peanut oil**

3–4 **garlic cloves**, finely chopped

1 tablespoon finely grated fresh **ginger**

2 small **red chillies**, seeded and finely chopped

1 1/2 tablespoons freshly ground **black pepper**

2 **spring onions (scallions)**, green part only, thinly sliced on the diagonal

Combine the soy sauces, oyster sauce and brown sugar in a small bowl or jug.

Freeze the crabs for 2–3 hours to immobilize them, if necessary, then wash them well with a stiff brush. Pull back the apron from the underside and remove the top shell from each crab (it should come off easily in one piece). Remove the intestine and grey, feathery gills. Cut the crab lengthways through the centre of the body, then cut in half again, crossways. Crack the claws with the back of a knife or cleaver.

Heat a wok over very high heat, add 1 tablespoon of the oil and swirl to coat. When the oil is just starting to smoke, add the crab pieces in batches and stir-fry over high heat for 6–8 minutes, or until the shells become bright orange — use a little more oil if necessary. Remove each batch from the wok.

Reduce the heat to medium, add the remaining oil and stir-fry the garlic, ginger, chilli and pepper for 30 seconds, or until fragrant. Add the combined sauces and simmer for about 1 minute, or until glossy. Return the crab to the wok, cover and cook, stirring every minute for 6–8 minutes, or until cooked. Scatter with spring onion and serve.

coriander bamboo beef

serves 4 as part of a spread

6 **coriander (cilantro) roots and stems**

2 **garlic cloves**, crushed

1 tablespoon **whole black peppercorns**, dry roasted and crushed

2 tablespoons **fish sauce**

3 tablespoons **vegetable oil**

500 g (1 lb 2 oz) **beef fillet** or **rump steak**, thinly sliced

250 g (9 oz/1 cup) sliced **bamboo shoots**

2 tablespoons chopped **coriander (cilantro) leaves**

Combine the coriander roots and stems, garlic, pepper, 1 tablespoon of fish sauce and 1 tablespoon of oil in a food processor and blend until a smooth paste forms. Put the beef in a non-metallic bowl, add the marinade and mix well. Cover and marinate in the refrigerator for 2 hours.

Heat a wok over high heat, add another tablespoon of oil and swirl to coat. Add the bamboo shoots and stir-fry for 1 minute, then stir in the remaining fish sauce and cook for an additional minute. Remove and set aside. Heat the remaining oil, add the beef in batches and stir-fry for 3–4 minutes, or until browned. Return the bamboo shoots to the wok, then toss to combine with the beef. Remove from the heat, stir in the coriander leaves and serve immediately.

balinese-style nasi goreng

serves 4

3 tablespoons **vegetable** or **canola oil**

2 **eggs**, lightly beaten, seasoned with salt and white pepper

150 g (5½ oz) **snake beans**, finely chopped

250 ml (9 fl oz/1 cup) **vegetable** or **canola oil**, extra, for deep-frying

8 uncooked **prawn crackers**

3 **garlic cloves**, chopped

1 **onion** or 4 **red Asian shallots**, finely chopped

1 small **bird's eye chilli**

200 g (7 oz) **raw small prawns (shrimp)**, peeled and deveined

250 g (9 oz) **chicken breast fillet**, thinly sliced

740 g (1 lb 10 oz/4 cups) steamed **long-grain rice** (see tip)

4 **spring onions (scallions)**, finely sliced

1 tablespoon **kecap manis**

1–2 tablespoons **light soy sauce**

8 **iceberg lettuce leaves**, trimmed to form a bowl shape

1 **tomato**, sliced

1 small **cucumber**, seeded and thinly sliced

1 tablespoon **fried red Asian shallots**

Crush the garlic, onion and chilli to **a rough paste** in a mortar and pestle.

For really **fresh prawn crackers** buy uncooked ones and deep-fry them as you need them.

Heat 1 tablespoon of oil in a wok over medium heat, add the beaten egg and swirl over the base to create an omelette. Cook over low heat for 3–5 minutes, or until set, then turn out onto a plate and slice thinly. Cook the beans in boiling water for 3 minutes, then drain and refresh under cold water.

In a small saucepan, heat the extra oil until very hot. Add two prawn crackers at a time and cook for 30 seconds, or until crisp. Drain on crumpled paper towels.

Crush the garlic, onion and chilli to a rough paste in a mortar and pestle or small food processor. Heat the remaining 2 tablespoons of oil in a wok, swirl to coat, and cook the paste for 1 minute, or until fragrant. Add the prawns and chicken, and stir-fry for 3 minutes, or until the prawns have turned pink. Add 2 tablespoons of water and the beans, and season with salt and freshly ground black pepper. Add the cooked rice, spring onion, kecap manis and soy sauce, stirring continuously until all the ingredients are heated through.

To serve, put two lettuce leaves on each serving plate and divide the filling among them. Garnish with slices of tomato and cucumber, and top with sliced omelette, broken prawn crackers and fried red Asian shallots.

tip You will need to cook 300 g (10½ oz/1½ cups) of long-grain rice to obtain 740 g (1 lb 10 oz/4 cups) of cooked rice. This dish is often served with peanut sauce and fried garlic.

chilli and tofu stir-fry

serves 6

3 tablespoons **peanut oil**

1 teaspoon bottled **crushed chilli**

2 teaspoons grated fresh **ginger**

2 **garlic cloves**, crushed

250 g (9 oz) **hard tofu**, cut into 1.5 cm (5/8 inch) cubes

8 **spring onions (scallions)**, sliced on the diagonal

150 g (51/2 oz) fresh **baby corn**, halved lengthways

150 g (51/2 oz) **snowpeas (mangetout)**, topped and tailed

500 g (1 lb 2 oz) **hokkien (egg) noodles**

40 g (11/2 oz/1/4 cup) **cashew nuts**

2 tablespoons **soy sauce**

125 ml (4 fl oz/1/2 cup) **vegetable stock**

1 handful **coriander (cilantro) leaves**

Heat the oil in a wok over medium heat and swirl to coat. Add the chilli, ginger and garlic and stir-fry for about 2–3 minutes, or until aromatic. Add the tofu cubes, spring onion and baby corn and stir-fry for 2–3 minutes.

Add the snowpeas, noodles and cashews and cook, stirring, for 3–5 minutes, or until the vegetables are almost tender. Stir in the soy sauce and stock, then bring to the boil and simmer for 2 minutes, or until slightly reduced. Stir in the coriander and serve immediately.

tip Serve on a large platter lined with banana leaves if available.

japanese sake beef stir-fry

serves 3–4

1½ tablespoons toasted **sesame seeds**

600 g (1 lb 5 oz) **rump steak**, thinly sliced

2 **garlic cloves**, finely chopped

2 teaspoons grated fresh **ginger**

3 **spring onions (scallions)**, finely chopped

1 teaspoon **soft brown sugar**

100 ml (3½ fl oz) **Japanese soy sauce**

a few drops of **sesame oil**

3 tablespoons **mirin**

3 tablespoons **sake**

1–2 tablespoons **vegetable oil**

4 **spring onions (scallions)**, extra, diagonally sliced into 3 cm (1¼ inch) pieces

Put 1 tablespoon of sesame seeds in a mortar and pestle and grind to a powder. Put the beef slices in a large non-metallic bowl. In a separate bowl combine the garlic, ginger, spring onion, sugar, ground sesame seeds, 1 tablespoon of the soy sauce and a few drops of sesame oil. Pour this mixture over the beef and mix gently to coat. Season with freshly ground black pepper, cover and marinate for 2 hours in the refrigerator.

Drain the beef well, reserving the marinade. Add the mirin, sake and remaining soy sauce to the marinade and set aside.

Heat a wok over high heat, add 1 tablespoon of oil and swirl to coat. Stir-fry the beef in batches for 1 minute, or until just starting to brown (add more oil between batches if necessary). Remove and keep warm.

Pour the marinade into the wok, bring to the boil, then simmer for 3–4 minutes, or until reduced by half. Return the beef to the wok, stirring quickly for 1–2 minutes, or until it is heated through and well coated with the sauce. Serve garnished with the remaining sesame seeds and sliced spring onion.

yangzhou-style fried rice

serves 4

2 tablespoons **dried shrimp**

3 tablespoons **vegetable oil**

3 **eggs**, lightly beaten

250 g (9 oz) **Chinese barbecue pork**, finely diced

100 g (3½ oz/½ cup) **tinned straw mushrooms**, drained, rinsed and finely diced

740 g (1 lb 10 oz/4 cups) cooked **long-grain rice**, cold (see tip)

2½ tablespoons **light soy sauce**

3 **spring onions (scallions)**, finely chopped

2 tablespoons finely chopped **garlic chives**

white pepper, to taste

sesame oil, to taste

Put the dried shrimp in a small heatproof bowl and cover with boiling water. Leave to soak for 15 minutes, then drain and finely chop.

Heat a wok until very hot, add 1 tablespoon of oil and swirl to coat. Add the egg and leave it until it just starts to set. When the egg is almost cooked, break it into small strips with the edge of a spatula, then remove from the wok. Heat another tablespoon of oil in the wok, add the barbecue pork and stir-fry over high heat for 1 minute, or until heated through. Add the straw mushrooms and soaked shrimp, and continue to stir-fry with the pork for an additional 1–2 minutes.

Add the remaining oil, then gradually add the cooked rice, tossing and stirring for 2 minutes, or until heated through. Reduce the heat to medium, add the soy sauce, spring onion and garlic chives, then continue to stir-fry until all the ingredients are thoroughly combined and the soy sauce evenly coats the rice. Season to taste with white pepper and a drizzle of sesame oil, and serve immediately, topped with the omelette strips.

tip You will need to cook 300 g (10½ oz/1½ cups) of long-grain rice to obtain this amount of cooked rice.

stir-fried squid flowers with capsicum

serves 4

400 g (14 oz) **squid tubes**

3 tablespoons **oil**

2 tablespoons **salted fermented black beans**, mashed

1 small **onion**, cut into small cubes

1 small **green capsicum (pepper)**, cut into small cubes

3–4 small slices fresh **ginger**

1 **spring onion (scallion)**, cut into short lengths

1 small **red chilli**, chopped

1 tablespoon **Chinese rice wine**

1/2 teaspoon **roasted sesame oil**

Open up the squid tubes and scrub off any soft jelly-like substance, then score the inside of the flesh with a fine criss-cross pattern, making sure you do not cut all the way through. Cut the squid into 3 x 5 cm (1¼ x 2 inch) pieces.

Blanch the squid in a saucepan of boiling water for 25–30 seconds — each piece will curl up and the criss-cross pattern will open out, hence the name 'squid flower'. Remove and refresh in cold water, then drain and dry well.

Heat a wok over high heat, add the oil and heat until very hot. Stir-fry the black beans, onion, capsicum, ginger, spring onion and chilli for about 1 minute. Add the squid and rice wine, mix well and stir for 1 minute. Sprinkle with the sesame oil and serve immediately.

three mushroom ginger chicken

serves 3–4

500 g (1 lb 2 oz) **chicken breast fillet**, thinly sliced

1 tablespoon **Scotch whisky**

1 tablespoon **light soy sauce**

15 g (1/2 oz) **dried black** or **wood ear fungus**

3 tablespoons **peanut oil**

2 tablespoons finely julienned fresh **ginger**

2 **spring onions (scallions)**, cut into 3 cm (11/4 inch) lengths

1 small **red capsicum (pepper)**, finely sliced

150 g (51/2 oz) fresh **shiitake mushrooms**, stems removed, finely sliced

150 g (51/2 oz) fresh **oyster mushrooms**, finely sliced

1 **garlic clove**, crushed

3 tablespoons **mushroom oyster sauce** or **oyster sauce**

1 tablespoon **mushroom soy sauce**

1/2 teaspoon ground **white pepper**

Put the chicken in a non-metallic bowl with the whisky and light soy sauce. Mix to coat, then cover and marinate in the refrigerator for 1 hour. Meanwhile, soak the fungus in boiling water for 20 minutes. Rinse, then finely slice.

Drain the chicken well. Heat a wok over high heat, add 1 tablespoon of the oil and swirl to coat. Stir-fry the chicken in batches for 2–3 minutes, or until golden brown and tender. Remove and keep warm.

Heat the remaining oil, then add the fungus, ginger, spring onion, capsicum and mushrooms and stir-fry for 1–2 minutes, or until the vegetables are soft. Return the chicken to the wok with the garlic and stir-fry for 1 minute. Add the mushroom oyster sauce, soy sauce and white pepper and stir to combine, cooking for an additional minute until the chicken is cooked through and coated with the sauce.

vegetarian san choy bau

serves 4

6 **dried shiitake mushrooms**

8 large **iceberg lettuce leaves**

1 tablespoon **dark soy sauce**

2 tablespoons **hoisin sauce**

2 tablespoons **Chinese rice wine**

1/2 teaspoon **sugar**

1/2 teaspoon **sesame oil**

1 teaspoon **cornflour (cornstarch)**, mixed with 1 teaspoon cold water

1 tablespoon **vegetable** or **peanut oil**

5 **spring onions (scallions)**, finely chopped

2 **garlic cloves**, crushed

1 tablespoon finely grated fresh **ginger**

2 tablespoons finely chopped **coriander (cilantro) stems**

125 g (41/2 oz) packet **fried tofu puffs**, shredded

300 g (101/2 oz/4 cups) shredded **cabbage**

110 g (33/4 oz/2/3 cup) drained **water chestnuts**, chopped

1 handful **coriander (cilantro) leaves**

2 **spring onions (scallions)**, extra, sliced on the diagonal, to serve

hoisin sauce, extra, to serve

Soak the shiitake mushrooms in 125 ml (4 fl oz/1/2 cup) of hot water for 10 minutes. Wash the lettuce and dry well. Drain the mushrooms, reserving 2 tablespoons of the liquid, discard the woody stems and finely chop the caps. Combine the soy sauce, hoisin sauce, rice wine, reserved mushroom liquid, sugar, sesame oil and cornflour mixture.

Heat a wok over high heat. Add the oil and swirl to coat. Cook the spring onion, garlic, ginger and coriander stems for 1 minute. Add the tofu and cook for 1 minute. Add the mushrooms, cabbage and water chestnuts and cook for 2–3 minutes, or until the cabbage has wilted.

Pour in the combined soy sauce mixture and cook for 1 minute. Add the coriander leaves and toss to combine. Divide the mixture among the lettuce cups, garnish with spring onion and drizzle with the extra hoisin sauce.

hokkien mee

serves 6

500 g (1 lb 2 oz) **hokkien (egg) noodles**

3 tablespoons **peanut oil**

2 **garlic cloves**, crushed

1 teaspoon **sambal oelek**

200 g (7 oz) **Chinese barbecue pork**, thinly sliced

3 **Chinese sausages (lap cheong)**, steamed and sliced diagonally

375 g (13 oz/1 bunch) **baby bok choy (pak choy)**, leaves separated

180 g (6 oz/2 cups) **bean sprouts**, tails trimmed

2 tablespoons **oyster sauce**

2 tablespoons **dark soy sauce**

2 **eggs**, lightly beaten

125–150 ml (4–5 fl oz) **chicken stock**

200 g (7 oz/2 bunches) **garlic chives**, snipped

lemon wedges, to serve

Put the hokkien noodles in a heatproof bowl, cover with boiling water and soak for 1 minute. Drain, rinse and set aside until needed.

Heat a wok over high heat, add 1 tablespoon of oil and swirl to coat. Stir in the garlic and sambal oelek and cook for 30 seconds, or until fragrant. Add the barbecue pork and Chinese sausage and stir-fry quickly for 1 minute. Add the bok choy and stir-fry for 1 minute, or until it starts to wilt. Add the bean sprouts, noodles, oyster sauce and dark soy sauce to the wok and stir-fry for 3–4 minutes.

Push the ingredients to one side of the wok, then add the remaining oil and pour in the beaten egg. Stir to scramble, then as the eggs start to cook, toss to combine with the other ingredients. Add the stock and garlic chives and stir until well combined. Serve immediately with lemon wedges on the side.

thai basil, beef and asparagus stir-fry

serves 3–4

3 tablespoons **peanut oil**

500 g (1 lb 2 oz) **beef fillet** or **rump steak**, thinly sliced

2 **garlic cloves**, crushed

1 small **red chilli**, finely chopped

175 g (6 oz/1 bunch) **asparagus**, trimmed and sliced
   diagonally into thirds

1 large handful **Thai basil leaves**

1 tablespoon **fish sauce**

1 tablespoon **oyster sauce**

Thai basil leaves, extra, to serve

Heat a wok over high heat, add 1 tablespoon of the oil and swirl to coat. Stir-fry the beef in batches for 2–3 minutes, or until almost cooked through — add more oil if necessary. Remove and keep warm.

Heat the remaining oil. Add the garlic, chilli and asparagus and stir-fry for 1 minute. Return the beef to the wok. Toss in the basil, then add the fish sauce, oyster sauce and freshly ground black pepper to taste and stir-fry for 1 minute, or until the beef is heated through. Garnish with the extra basil leaves and serve immediately.

scallops in black bean sauce

serves 4

2 tablespoons **oil**

32 **scallops**, rinsed and drained very well, roe discarded

1 tablespoon **salted fermented black beans**

1 tablespoon **soy sauce**

2 tablespoons **Chinese rice wine**

1 teaspoon **sugar**

1 **garlic clove**, finely chopped

1 **spring onion (scallion)**, finely chopped

1/2 teaspoon finely grated fresh **ginger**

1 teaspoon **sesame oil**

1 **spring onion (scallion)**, extra, thinly sliced on the diagonal

Heat 1 tablespoon of the oil in a wok and swirl to coat. When hot, add the scallops (in batches if necessary) and cook over high heat for 2 minutes, or until firm. Transfer to a plate and drain to remove any excess liquid.

Wash the black beans thoroughly under cold running water. Mix together the soy sauce, rice wine, sugar and 1 tablespoon of water in a cup.

Add the remaining oil to the wok and heat until it begins to smoke. Add the garlic, spring onion and ginger and cook for 30 seconds. Add the beans and the soy sauce mixture and bring to the boil.

Return the scallops to the sauce with the sesame oil and simmer for 30 seconds. Serve immediately, garnished with the extra spring onion.

sticky tamarind lamb

serves 2

2 tablespoons **lime juice**

1 tablespoon **tamarind concentrate**

1 tablespoon **fish sauce**

2 tablespoons **peanut oil**

500 g (1 lb 2 oz) **lean lamb sirloin** or **backstrap fillets**, thinly sliced

150 g (5½ oz) **sugar snap peas**, trimmed

3 **red Asian shallots**, finely chopped

2 **garlic cloves**, crushed

2 tablespoons toasted **unsalted peanuts**, crushed

Combine the lime juice, tamarind concentrate and fish sauce in a small non-metallic bowl or jug.

Heat a wok over high heat, add 1 tablespoon of oil and swirl to coat. Stir-fry the lamb in batches for 2–3 minutes, or until well browned. Remove and keep warm. Heat the remaining oil in the wok, then quickly stir-fry the sugar snap peas for about 1 minute, or until tender. Remove from the wok.

Add the shallots and garlic to the wok and stir-fry for 30 seconds, or until fragrant. Stir in the tamarind mixture, bring it to the boil and simmer for 2–3 minutes, or until reduced to a thick, sticky syrup. Return the lamb and sugar snap peas to the wok and toss to coat well with the sauce. Serve garnished with crushed peanuts.

phad thai

serves 4

10 raw **tiger prawns** or 20 **small prawns**
  (shrimp), peeled and deveined
200 g (7 oz) **medium-thickness dried**
  rice noodles
1 tablespoon **dried shrimp**
3 tablespoons **vegetable oil**
2 large **eggs**, lightly beaten
2 **garlic cloves**, crushed
1 small **red chilli**, finely chopped
2 tablespoons grated **palm sugar**
  or **soft brown sugar**

3 tablespoons **lemon juice**
2 tablespoons **fish sauce**
4 tablespoons **peanuts**, toasted and
  roughly chopped
3 **spring onions (scallions)**, sliced on
  the diagonal
90 g (3¼ oz/1 cup) **bean sprouts**,
  tails trimmed
3 tablespoons **coriander (cilantro)**
  leaves
lemon wedges, to serve

If using tiger prawns, chop each one into three or four pieces, depending on size. Put the rice noodles in a bowl and cover with boiling water. Put the dried shrimp in a cup and cover with boiling water. Leave both to soak for 10 minutes, then drain. Make sure you have all the other ingredients at the ready before you start cooking.

Heat the oil in a wok over high heat until smoking. Add the beaten egg and cook for 30 seconds, then stir to break into small pieces. Add the garlic, chilli and prawns and cook for 15 seconds, stirring all the time.

Add the sugar, lemon juice and fish sauce and cook for 15 seconds, stirring and tossing in the wok. Tip in the noodles, dried shrimp and 3 tablespoons of the peanuts. Toss together in the wok to heat through before adding the spring onion and bean sprouts. Cook for a further 30 seconds, then tip onto a serving plate and scatter the coriander and remaining peanuts over the top. Serve immediately with the lemon wedges.

tip To make this dish vegetarian, omit the prawns, shrimp paste and fish sauce. Replace the prawns with 250 g (9 oz) tofu puffs, adding them to the wok at the same time as the garlic and chilli. Replace the fish sauce with 1 tablespoon of soy sauce.

garlic chilli prawns

serves 4

1 tablespoon **peanut oil**

24 **raw king prawns (shrimp)**, peeled and deveined, tails intact

2 **garlic cloves**, finely chopped

1 small **red chilli**, seeded and finely chopped

1–2 tablespoons **chilli garlic sauce**

2 teaspoons **dark soy sauce**

sesame oil, for drizzling

2 **spring onions (scallions)**, green part only,
   cut diagonally into 3 cm (1¼ inch) lengths

Heat a wok over high heat, add the oil and swirl to coat. Add the prawns and the garlic and stir-fry for 1 minute, or until the prawns turn pink. Add the chilli, chilli garlic sauce and soy sauce and stir-fry for a further 2 minutes, or until the prawns are curled and glazed with the sauce. Drizzle with sesame oil, garnish with spring onion and serve.

sweet and sour pork

serves 6

sweet and sour sauce

1 tablespoon **oil**

1 **green capsicum (pepper)**, finely sliced

75 g (2¹/2 oz/¹/3 cup) **sugar**

3 tablespoons **rice vinegar**

1¹/2 tablespoons **light soy sauce**

1¹/2 tablespoons **tomato paste (purée)**

¹/4 teaspoon **sesame oil**

4 tablespoons **chicken stock**

3 teaspoons **cornflour (cornstarch)**

2 **eggs**, lightly beaten

100 g (3¹/2 oz) **cornflour (cornstarch)**

900 g (2 lb) piece centre-cut **pork loin**, cut into 2 cm (³/4 inch) cubes

oil, for deep-frying

To make the sauce, heat a wok over high heat, add the oil and swirl to coat. Add the capsicum and stir-fry for 1 minute. Add the sugar, rice vinegar, soy sauce, tomato paste, sesame oil and stock and bring to the boil, stirring. Combine the cornflour with 1 tablespoon of water and stir to form a smooth paste. Add the mixture to the sauce and bring to the boil, stirring, until the sauce thickens. Remove from the heat and keep warm.

Mix together the beaten egg, cornflour and 3 teaspoons of cold water in a large bowl. Add the pork and toss until well coated in the mixture.

Fill a wok two-thirds full of oil and heat to 180°C (350°F), or until a cube of bread dropped in the oil browns in 15 seconds. Add the pork in batches and cook for 3–4 minutes, or until golden brown and crispy. Drain on paper towels. Remove the oil from the wok and wipe clean. Return the sauce to the wok and heat through for about 1 minute. Add the pork, toss well to coat and serve.

char kway teow with crab

serves 4

150 g (5 1/2 oz) **dried thin rice noodles**

3 tablespoons **vegetable** or **peanut oil**

2 **red Asian** or **French shallots**, thinly sliced

1 **garlic clove**, finely chopped

2 small **red chillies**, finely chopped

180 g (6 oz/2 cups) **bean sprouts**, tails trimmed

175 g (6 oz) **Chinese barbecue pork** or
   other cooked pork, cut into small pieces

3 tablespoons **light soy sauce**

2 tablespoons **oyster sauce**

700 g (1 lb 9 oz) fresh or thawed frozen **crab meat**

2 tablespoons chopped **coriander (cilantro) leaves**

Put the rice noodles in a bowl and cover with boiling water. Leave to soak for about 10 minutes, then drain.

Heat the oil in a wok and swirl to coat. When hot, add the shallots, garlic and chilli. Cook over high heat, stirring, for 2–3 minutes. Add the bean sprouts and pork pieces and cook for 2 minutes. Add the soy sauce, oyster sauce, noodles, crab meat and coriander and stir for 2 minutes, or until heated through. Add salt to taste and serve immediately.

lemon grass beef noodle bowl

serves 4

dressing

125 ml (4 fl oz/1/2 cup) **lime juice**

4 tablespoons **fish sauce**

1 tablespoon **caster (superfine) sugar**

4 tablespoons **warm water**

1–2 small **red chillies**, finely chopped

1 small **garlic clove**, finely chopped

marinade

3 stems **lemon grass**, white part only, finely chopped

2 **garlic cloves**, crushed

1 tablespoon **fish sauce**

1 tablespoon **light soy sauce**

2 teaspoons **caster (superfine) sugar**

1 teaspoon **vegetable oil**

500 g (1 lb 2 oz) **beef fillet** or **rump steak**, thinly sliced

240 g (81/2 oz) **dried rice vermicelli**

1–2 tablespoons **peanut oil**

1 small **Lebanese (short) cucumber**, seeded and julienned

1 small **carrot**, julienned

150 g (51/2 oz/12/3 cups) **bean sprouts**, tails trimmed

1 handful **coriander (cilantro) leaves**

1 small handful **Vietnamese mint leaves**, plus extra to serve

70 g (21/2 oz/1/2 cup) ground **unsalted toasted peanuts**, to serve

To make the dressing, combine all the ingredients in a non-metallic jug or bowl, stirring until the sugar has completely dissolved. Cover and set aside until required.

To make the marinade, put all the ingredients in a small food processor and pulse to form a smooth paste. Put the beef slices in a non-metallic bowl, cover with the marinade and stir to make sure the meat is completely coated. Cover with plastic wrap and marinate in the refrigerator for at least 2 hours.

When you are nearly ready to serve, soak the rice vermicelli in boiling water for 5 minutes. Drain, rinse and drain again.

Heat a wok over high heat, add 1 tablespoon of the oil and swirl to coat. Add the beef in batches and sear for 2–3 minutes, or until it is cooked to your liking (use extra oil if necessary). Remove from the heat.

Put the vermicelli in a large bowl, then add the cucumber, carrot, bean sprouts, coriander and mint leaves. Pour on the dressing and toss to combine all the ingredients thoroughly. Divide the noodle salad among four large, deep serving bowls, then top each with a quarter of the beef. Sprinkle the peanuts over the top and garnish with Vietnamese mint leaves. Serve immediately.

tip The noodle salad can be prepared a few hours in advance; however the dressing should not be added until you are ready to serve, otherwise the noodles absorb it and the salad will lose its flavour.

A pungent-tasting herb, **Vietnamese mint** resembles coriander rather than mint in **flavour**.

Stir the dressing well **to dissolve** the sugar.

lacy eggnets filled with mixed mushrooms

serves 6 as part of a spread

4 **eggs**

vegetable or **groundnut oil**, for frying

2 **garlic cloves**, chopped

100 g (3½ oz/1 punnet) fresh **shiitake mushrooms**, sliced

150 g (5½ oz) **oyster mushrooms**, sliced

125 g (4½ oz) **button mushrooms**, sliced

100 g (3½ oz/1 punnet) **enoki mushrooms**

2 **French** or **red Asian shallots**, finely sliced

2 tablespoons **oyster sauce**

2 teaspoons **soy sauce**

2 teaspoons **sugar**

1 tablespoon chopped **coriander (cilantro) leaves**

Lightly beat the eggs with 3 tablespoons of water, and strain into a wide bowl through a fine sieve to remove any membrane and lumps. Set aside while you make the filling.

To make the filling, heat a wok over medium–high heat. Add 2 tablespoons of oil, then add the garlic and all the mushrooms, except the enoki. Stir-fry for 1 minute, or until softened, then add the enoki mushrooms, shallots, oyster sauce and soy sauce, sugar and coriander. Stir-fry until combined, then remove the mixture from the wok and keep warm.

Clean the wok, then add 1–2 teaspoons of oil and heat over medium heat, swirling to coat the wok. Dip one hand into the egg mixture, then move it over the wok and let it drizzle through your fingers, quickly waving it across the oil. Do this a few times until the egg looks lacy. When the egg is set, carefully remove it and drain on paper towels. Repeat with the remaining egg mixture to make six nets in all. It might take a bit of trial and error to get the technique right.

Put one net on a board and spoon some of the filling on the bottom third. Carefully roll up the net, enclosing the sides to encase the filling. Repeat with the remaining nets and filling. Serve hot.

chilli mint lamb

serves 4

2 tablespoons **peanut oil**

500 g (1 lb 2 oz) **lamb sirloin** or **backstrap fillets**, thinly sliced

150 g (5¹/2 oz) **snake beans**, cut into 3 cm (1¹/4 inch) lengths

2 **garlic cloves**, crushed

1 small **red chilli**, finely sliced (seeded optional)

1¹/2 tablespoons **fish sauce**

1¹/2 tablespoons **lime juice**

1 teaspoon **chilli garlic sauce**

2 teaspoons grated **palm sugar**

1 handful **mint leaves**, plus extra to serve

Heat a wok over high heat, add 1 tablespoon of oil and swirl to coat. Stir-fry the lamb in batches for 2–3 minutes, or until browned. Remove and set aside.

Heat the remaining oil in the wok, add the snake beans and stir-fry for 1 minute, then add the garlic and chilli and toss for 30 seconds. Return the lamb to the wok with the fish sauce, lime juice, chilli garlic sauce and sugar. Stir-fry for 1–2 minutes, or until the lamb is heated through and coated with the sauce. Remove from the heat, gently stir in the mint and serve, garnished with extra mint leaves.

chicken larb in banana blossom

serves 4

1 tablespoon **vegetable oil**

400 g (14 oz) **minced (ground) chicken**

4 tablespoons **chicken stock**

1 stem **lemon grass**, white part only, finely chopped

1 **makrut (kaffir lime) leaf**, shredded

1½ tablespoons **fish sauce**

4 tablespoons **lime juice**

2 **spring onions (scallions)**, chopped

3 **red Asian shallots**, finely sliced

1 large handful **coriander (cilantro) leaves**, shredded

1 handful **mint**, shredded

1 small **red chilli**, seeded and finely chopped

4 **banana blossom leaves**, washed and dried

3 tablespoons **crisp fried shallots**

lime wedges, to serve

Heat a wok over medium heat, add the oil and swirl to coat. Add the chicken and stir-fry for 3–4 minutes, or until well browned. Add the stock, lemon grass, lime leaf and 1 tablespoon of fish sauce and simmer for 5 minutes. Remove from the heat.

Allow to cool, then stir in the lime juice, remaining fish sauce, spring onion, shallots, coriander, mint and chilli. Spoon the mixture into the banana blossom leaves, garnish with crisp fried shallots and serve with lime wedges on the side.

tip Don't eat the banana blossom leaves — they are purely for decorative purposes in this recipe.

chilli pork with cashews

serves 4

2–3 tablespoons **peanut oil**

600 g (1 lb 5 oz) **pork fillet**, thinly sliced

4 **spring onions (scallions)**, cut into 3 cm (1¼ inch) lengths

50 g (1¾ oz/⅓ cup) toasted **unsalted cashews**

1 tablespoon **fish sauce**

1 tablespoon **mushroom oyster sauce**

1–2 tablespoons **Thai chilli paste in soy bean oil** or **chilli jam**

1 large handful **Thai basil leaves**, plus extra to serve

Heat a wok over high heat, add 1 tablespoon of oil and swirl to coat. Stir-fry the pork in batches for 2–3 minutes, or until it starts to brown. Remove from the wok and keep warm.

Heat the remaining oil, then stir-fry the spring onion for 1 minute. Return the pork to the wok, along with any juices, and stir-fry for 2 minutes. Stir in the cashews, fish sauce, oyster sauce and chilli paste or jam. Toss for a further 2 minutes, or until the pork is tender and coated with the sauce. Remove from the heat and gently stir in the basil. Serve garnished with extra basil.

shaking beef

serves 4

750 g (1 lb 10 oz) **beef eye fillet**

1 tablespoon **fish sauce**

1 tablespoon **light soy sauce**

1 teaspoon **caster (superfine) sugar**

3–4 **garlic cloves**, crushed

2 **spring onions (scallions)**, white part only, finely chopped

1/2 teaspoon freshly ground **black pepper**

2 tablespoons **peanut oil**

100 g (3½ oz) **mixed frisée** and **red oak lettuce leaves**

Cut the beef into 2 cm (¾ inch) cubes and put them in a non-metallic bowl. Put the fish sauce, soy sauce, sugar, garlic, spring onion, black pepper and 1 teaspoon of the oil in a small jug, mix well and pour over the beef. Toss to coat the beef well, then cover and marinate in the refrigerator for at least 1 hour.

Heat a wok over high heat, add 1 tablespoon of oil and swirl to coat. When the oil is hot, add half the beef in one layer, allowing it to sit without tossing for 1 minute, so that a brown crust forms on the bottom. Stir-fry the beef quickly or use the wok handle to shake the beef vigorously, tossing it around the wok for 3–4 minutes for medium rare or longer if desired. Remove and repeat with the remaining oil and beef. Arrange the beef on a bed of salad leaves and serve.

asian vegetables

serves 4

30 g (1 oz) **lily buds** (see tip)

20 g (3/4 oz) fresh **black fungus (wood ears)**

8 large **dried shiitake mushrooms**

2 tablespoons **vegetable** or **peanut oil**

2 **garlic cloves**, chopped

1/2 **red capsicum (pepper)**, sliced

200 g (7 oz) tin **fried gluten**, drained (see tip)

2 1/2 tablespoons **oyster sauce**

2 teaspoons **soy sauce**

1 teaspoon **sugar**

Soak the lily buds and black fungus separately in warm water for 15 minutes, then drain. Soak the dried shiitake mushrooms in 125 ml (4 fl oz/1/2 cup) of hot water for 10 minutes. Drain. Discard the woody stems and chop the caps in half.

Heat the oil in a wok over medium heat. Add the garlic and capsicum and stir-fry for 1 minute. Add the lily buds, black fungus, mushrooms and gluten. Toss well for another minute. Stir in the oyster sauce, soy sauce and sugar and mix gently until combined. Delicious served with steamed rice.

tips Lily buds (also known as golden needles) are the unopened flowers of day lilies. The buds are usually bought dried and then soaked, but are sometimes available fresh from Chinese markets. They have an earthy flavour and are used mainly in Chinese vegetarian dishes, or in stir-fries. Fried gluten is sold in tins or bottles in Asian shops, and is usually used as a substitute for meat, due to its 'meaty' texture.

lamb stir-fry with orange and sichuan pepper

serves 3–4

2 tablespoons **soy sauce**

125 ml (4 fl oz/1/2 cup) **orange juice**

1/4 teaspoon **bicarbonate of soda**

2 teaspoons **cornflour (cornstarch)**

2 teaspoons crushed **Sichuan peppercorns**

3 tablespoons **peanut oil**

350 g (12 oz) **lamb fillet**, thinly sliced

5 cm (2 inch) piece fresh **ginger**, julienned

4 **star anise**

10 thin **spring onions (scallions)**, cut into 2.5 cm (1 inch) lengths

2 **garlic cloves**, crushed

200 g (7 oz) **snowpeas (mangetout)**, topped and tailed, cut on the diagonal

2 small **red chillies**, finely sliced

2 tablespoons **oyster sauce**

2 tablespoons **Chinese rice wine**

1/2 teaspoon **sugar**

coconut rice

400 ml (14 fl oz) **coconut milk**

200 g (7 oz/1 cup) **basmati rice**

Put the soy sauce, orange juice, bicarbonate of soda, cornflour, peppercorns and 1 tablespoon of oil in a bowl. Add the lamb and mix well. Marinate, covered, in the refrigerator for 30 minutes. Drain, reserving the marinade.

Meanwhile, prepare the coconut rice. Mix the coconut milk with 375 ml (13 fl oz/ 11/2 cups) of water and 1 teaspoon of salt in a large saucepan. Stir in the rice, bring to the boil, then reduce the heat and simmer for 15 minutes. Remove from the heat and cover with a tea towel under the lid for 5 minutes to finish cooking through.

Heat a wok over high heat, add 1 tablespoon of oil and stir-fry the lamb in batches for 1–2 minutes, or until just seared. Remove and set aside. Heat the remaining oil, add the ginger, star anise, spring onion, garlic, snowpeas and chilli and stir-fry for 30 seconds. Return the lamb to the wok with the reserved marinade and the combined oyster sauce, rice wine and sugar. Stir-fry for 1 minute, then serve with the coconut rice.

tip Put the lamb in the freezer for 30 minutes before cutting into thin slices.

clams in yellow bean sauce

serves 4

1.5 kg (3 lb 5 oz) **clams (vongole)**

1 tablespoon **oil**

2 **garlic cloves**, crushed

1 tablespoon grated fresh **ginger**

2 tablespoons **yellow bean sauce (taucheo)**

125 ml (4 fl oz/1/2 cup) **chicken stock**

1 **spring onion (scallion)**, finely chopped

Wash the clams in several changes of cold water, leaving them for a few minutes each time to remove any grit. Scrub the clams well, discarding any that remain open. Drain well.

Heat the wok until very hot, add the oil and stir-fry the garlic and ginger for 30 seconds. Add the yellow bean sauce and clams, and toss together. Add the stock and stir until the clams have all opened, discarding any that do not open after 3 minutes. Season with salt and white pepper.

Transfer the clams to a plate, garnish with the spring onion and serve.

tip You can use any variety of clam for this recipe; just make sure they are not too large and that they are very clean.

chicken with almonds and asparagus

serves 4

4 tablespoons **peanut oil**

50 g (1¾ oz/⅓ cup) **blanched almonds**

2 teaspoons **cornflour (cornstarch)**

4 tablespoons **chicken stock**

½ teaspoon **sesame oil**

2 tablespoons **oyster sauce**

1 tablespoon **soy sauce**

3 **garlic cloves**, crushed

1 teaspoon finely chopped fresh **ginger**

¼ teaspoon **white pepper**

1 **onion**, cut into wedges

500 g (1 lb 2 oz) **chicken thigh fillet**, cut into 3 x 2 cm (1¼ x ¾ inch) strips

1 **carrot**, cut into half moons

175 g (6 oz/1 bunch) **thin asparagus**, trimmed and cut into 3 cm (1¼ inch) lengths

60 g (2¼ oz/¼ cup) fresh **bamboo shoots**, cut into 1 cm (½ inch) dice

Whole **bamboo shoots** can be bought from Asian supermarkets.

Keep the food constantly moving, using **a tossing action** with a charn.

Heat 1 tablespoon of the peanut oil in a wok over high heat, add the almonds and stir-fry until golden. Drain on paper towels.

Combine the cornflour and stock in a small bowl, then stir in the sesame oil, oyster sauce, soy sauce, garlic, ginger and white pepper.

Heat 1 tablespoon of the peanut oil in the wok over high heat until smoking. Add half the onion and half the chicken strips and stir-fry for 2–3 minutes, or until the chicken is almost cooked through. Remove from the wok. Repeat with another tablespoon of oil and the remaining onion and chicken.

Add the remaining peanut oil to the wok and heat until just smoking. Add the carrot and stir-fry over high heat for 1–2 minutes, or until just starting to brown, then add the asparagus and the bamboo shoots, stir-frying for another minute. Remove the vegetables from the wok and set aside with the chicken.

Stir the cornflour mixture well then add to the wok. Stir over medium–high heat until the mixture thickens, then return the chicken and vegetables to the wok, stirring well to combine. Cook for a further 1–2 minutes, or until heated through. Remove to a serving dish and sprinkle with the almonds before serving.

curried eggplant stir-fry

serves 4 as a side dish

2 tablespoons **vegetable oil**

1/2–1 **long green chilli**, finely sliced

4 **red Asian shallots**, chopped

2 **garlic cloves**, finely sliced

2 tablespoons **rogan josh masala curry paste** or **mild curry paste**

350 g (12 oz) **slender eggplants (aubergines)**,
   cut on the diagonal into 1 cm (1/2 inch) slices

3 **vine-ripened tomatoes**, each cut into 8 wedges

70 g (21/2 oz/11/2 cups) **baby English spinach leaves**

Heat the oil in a large wok and swirl to coat. Add the green chilli, shallots and garlic and stir-fry over high heat for 1 minute. Stir in the curry paste and stir-fry for 1 minute.

Add the eggplant and stir-fry for 3 minutes, or until the eggplant has softened a little. Add the tomato and 125 ml (4 fl oz/1/2 cup) of water. Cover the wok and cook for 10 minutes, or until the eggplant is cooked, stirring occasionally. Stir in the spinach leaves and cook for 1 minute, or until wilted. Serve immediately.

lime and coconut udon noodles

serves 4 as a side dish

1 tablespoon **peanut oil**

1/2 teaspoon **sesame oil**

1 small **onion**, finely sliced

1 small **red chilli**, finely chopped

1 **garlic clove**, crushed

1 teaspoon freshly grated **ginger**

1 tablespoon **lime juice**

1 teaspoon **fish sauce**

1/2 teaspoon **sugar**

270 ml (9¹/2 fl oz) **coconut milk**

500 g (1 lb 2 oz) fresh **udon noodles**

1 small handful **coriander (cilantro) leaves**

crisp fried shallots (optional), to serve (see tip)

Heat the peanut and sesame oils in a wok and swirl to coat. Add the onion, chilli, garlic and ginger and stir-fry for over medium heat for 2–3 minutes, or until the onion is tender.

Add the combined lime juice, fish sauce, sugar and coconut milk, bring to a simmer and add the noodles. Cook, stirring, for 4–5 minutes, or until the mixture boils and thickens. Spoon into serving bowls and garnish with the coriander leaves and crisp fried shallots.

tip Crisp fried shallots can be bought ready-made from Asian supermarkets and some general supermarkets. If you can't find them, simply slice French or red Asian shallots very thinly and deep-fry in oil for about 30 seconds, or until crispy. Drain on paper towels.

mixed asian mushrooms with dashi

serves 4 as a side dish

1 teaspoon **dashi granules**

1 tablespoon **Japanese soy sauce**

1 tablespoon **mirin**

1 1/2 tablespoons **vegetable oil**

150 g (5 1/2 oz) **oyster mushrooms,** halved if large

300 g (10 1/2 oz/3 punnets) fresh **shiitake mushrooms,** sliced

300 g (10 1/2 oz/3 punnets) **enoki mushrooms,** separated into small bunches

1 teaspoon finely grated fresh **ginger**

1 **spring onion (scallion),** white part finely chopped, green part shredded

300 g (10 1/2 oz) **shimeji mushrooms,** separated

In a small bowl or jug, combine the dashi granules with 125 ml (4 fl oz/1/2 cup) of boiling water, then stir in the Japanese soy sauce and mirin.

Heat a wok over high heat, add 1 tablespoon of the oil and swirl to coat. Add the oyster, shiitake and enoki mushrooms in batches and stir-fry for 1–2 minutes, or until wilted and softened. Remove from the wok.

Heat the remaining oil in the wok, add the ginger and white part of the spring onion and stir-fry for 30 seconds, or until fragrant. Return the cooked mushrooms to the wok along with the dashi mixture and bring to the boil. Stir-fry for 1 minute, or until the mushrooms are heated through. Remove the wok from the heat, add the shimeji mushrooms and toss until wilted from the heat of the other mushrooms. Serve immediately, garnished with the spring onion greens.

soba noodles with sesame and soy

serves 4 as a side dish

sesame dressing

1 tablespoon **sesame oil**

2 tablespoons **light soy sauce**

2 tablespoons **mirin**

6 **dried shiitake mushrooms**

250 g (9 oz) **soba noodles**

1 tablespoon **sesame oil**

6 **spring onions (scallions)**, shredded into 5 cm (2 inch) strips

5 cm (2 inch) piece fresh **ginger**, cut into thin strips

2 **garlic cloves**, finely sliced

1 tablespoon toasted **sesame seeds**

mint leaves, to serve

To make the dressing, combine all the ingredients in a small jug.

Soak the mushrooms in 185 ml (6 fl oz/3/4 cup) of boiling water for 10 minutes. Drain, reserving 80 ml (2 1/2 fl oz/1/3 cup) of the water. Discard the woody stems and slice the caps finely.

Cook the soba noodles in boiling water for 3 minutes, or until tender. Drain.

Heat the oil in a large wok over medium heat and stir-fry the spring onion, ginger and garlic for 2 minutes. Add the mushrooms and soba noodles, stir to warm through, then add the sesame dressing and reserved mushroom water. Gently toss until the sauce has coated the noodles. Serve sprinkled with the sesame seeds and mint leaves.

indian stir-fried cauliflower with cashew nuts

serves 4 as a side dish

1 tablespoon **vegetable** or **peanut oil**

1 **onion**, cut into thin wedges

2 **garlic cloves**, crushed

1 tablespoon **Madras curry powder** or **mild curry powder**

2 teaspoons **mild curry paste**

500 g (1 lb 2 oz) **cauliflower**, cut into small florets

2 **tomatoes**, cut into wedges

125 ml (4 fl oz/1/2 cup) **chicken** or **vegetable stock**

2 teaspoons **tomato paste (purée)**

3 tablespoons **thick coconut cream**

100 g (31/2oz/2/3 cup) **unsalted toasted cashew nuts**, roughly chopped

coriander (cilantro) leaves, to garnish

Heat a wok over high heat, add the oil and swirl to coat. Add the onion and stir-fry for 1–2 minutes, or until golden. Add the garlic, curry powder and curry paste and stir-fry for 1 minute. Stir in the cauliflower and toss until well coated.

Add the tomato, stock, tomato paste and coconut cream and stir-fry for about 5–6 minutes, or until well combined and the cauliflower is cooked. Toss through the nuts just before serving and serve garnished with the coriander leaves.

chinese fried rice

serves 4 as a side dish

350 g (12 oz/1³/4 cups) **long-grain rice**

1 tablespoon **vegetable** or **peanut oil**

2 **eggs**, beaten

3 **Chinese sausages (lap cheong)**, thinly sliced on the diagonal (see tip)

100 g (3¹/2 oz) **snake beans**, cut into 2 cm (³/4 inch) lengths

6 **spring onions (scallions)**, finely chopped

2 **garlic cloves**, crushed

2 teaspoons grated fresh **ginger**

160 g (5¹/2 oz) small **raw prawns (shrimp)**, peeled and deveined

100 g (3¹/2 oz/²/3 cup) **frozen peas**, thawed

2 tablespoons **soy sauce**

2 **spring onions (scallions)**, extra, thinly sliced on the diagonal

Wash the rice under cold running water until the water runs clear. Bring a large saucepan of water to the boil, add the rice and cook for 10–12 minutes, or until tender. Drain and rinse under cold water to remove any excess starch. Spread out on a flat tray and refrigerate for 2 hours or preferably overnight.

Heat a wok over high heat, add half the oil and swirl to coat. Add the egg, swirling to coat the side of the wok. When the egg is almost set, roll it up in the wok, turn off the heat, then remove. Roughly chop and set aside.

Reheat the wok over high heat, add the remaining oil and swirl to coat. Add the Chinese sausage and snake beans and stir-fry for 2–3 minutes. Add the spring onion, garlic and ginger and stir-fry for 1 minute. Add the prawns and stir-fry for 1–2 minutes, or until cooked. Stir in the rice and peas and toss until well combined and heated through. Stir in the soy sauce and serve garnished with the chopped egg and extra spring onion.

tip Lap cheong is a Chinese dried pork sausage and can be found in the non-refrigerated section of Asian food stores. When using in a recipe, make sure it is thoroughly cooked, and refrigerate any remaining sausages after opening.

yin yang tofu with bean sprouts and garlic chives

serves 4 as a side dish

300 g (10¹/2 oz) packet **firm tofu**, cut into 1 cm (¹/2 inch) cubes

3 tablespoons **peanut oil**

90 g (3¹/4 oz/1 cup) **bean sprouts**, tails trimmed

1 **garlic clove**, crushed with a pinch of salt

1 tablespoon julienned fresh **ginger**

50 g (1³/4 oz) **garlic chives**, snipped into 3 cm (1¹/4 inch) lengths

3 tablespoons **kecap manis** (see tip)

2 tablespoons **chicken stock**

2 teaspoons **oyster sauce**

coriander (cilantro) sprigs, to serve

Carefully pat the tofu dry with paper towels (this prevents it from spitting when it is added to the hot oil). Heat a wok over high heat, add 2 tablespoons of the oil and swirl to coat. Add the tofu in batches and stir-fry for 2–3 minutes, taking care that it does not break up. Remove and set aside.

Heat the remaining oil, add the bean sprouts, garlic, ginger and garlic chives and stir-fry until the bean sprouts are tender but still firm. Return the tofu to the wok with the kecap manis, stock and oyster sauce and toss to combine. Cook for another minute or so, until the sauce coats the tofu. Garnish with the coriander.

tip Kecap manis is a thick, dark sweetened soy sauce made from black soy beans. It is available from Asian supermarkets. If you can't find it, stir a little brown sugar into soy sauce until dissolved.

stir-fried asparagus and beans

serves 4 as a side dish

1 tablespoon **vegetable oil**

4 **spring onions (scallions)**, chopped

2 **garlic cloves**, finely sliced

1 small **red chilli**, seeded and chopped

400 g (14 oz) **asparagus**, trimmed and cut on the diagonal into 5 cm (2 inch) pieces

300 g (10½ oz) **green beans**, trimmed and halved (or baby beans left whole)

2 tablespoons **oyster sauce**

1 tablespoon **fish sauce**

2 teaspoons shaved **palm sugar**

½ teaspoon **ground black pepper**

Heat the oil in a large wok over high heat and stir-fry the spring onion, garlic and chilli for 1 minute. Add the asparagus and beans and stir-fry for 1 minute.

Pour in 3 tablespoons of water, then steam, covered, for 3–4 minutes, or until the vegetables are just tender. Add the oyster sauce, fish sauce, palm sugar and black pepper. Stir until the sugar has dissolved, then serve immediately.

fragrant fish in betel leaves

makes 24

1 stem **lemon grass**, white part only, bruised

2 **makrut (kaffir lime) leaves**, torn

500 ml (17 fl oz/2 cups) **chicken stock**

400 g (14 oz) **blue eye cod fillet**

90 g (3¼ oz/1½ cups) shaved fresh coconut meat

1 small handful **Vietnamese mint**

2 tablespoons chopped **mint**

3 **red Asian shallots**, finely chopped

24 **betel leaves**, washed and dried (see tip)

180 g (6½ oz) **seaweed salad**, to garnish (see tip)

dressing

1 tablespoon **coconut vinegar**

1 tablespoon **lime juice**

3 teaspoons **fish sauce**

2 teaspoons **caster (superfine) sugar**

1 small **red chilli**, seeded and finely chopped

Put the lemon grass, lime leaves and stock in a wok over medium–high heat and bring to a simmer. Add the fish and poach gently, turning once, for 10–12 minutes, or until the fish is just cooked through and flakes easily with a fork. Remove and set aside to cool, discarding the broth.

To make the dressing, combine the ingredients in a small bowl or jug.

In a large non-metallic bowl, combine the coconut, mints and shallots. Gently flake the cooled fish into small pieces with a fork and add to the bowl. Pour on the dressing and stir gently until thoroughly combined. Put tablespoons of the fish salad on the betel leaves, garnish with seaweed salad and serve. To eat, roll up the leaves to enclose the filling.

tips Betel leaves are used frequently in Asian cuisine for wrapping food in. They are edible tender green leaves and are available in bunches from Asian food stores. Seaweed salad is available from good-quality seafood specialists.

quick vegetable stir-fry

serves 4 as a side dish

2 tablespoons **oil**

2 **garlic cloves**, finely chopped

2 teaspoons finely chopped fresh **ginger**

1 **carrot**, sliced

1 **red capsicum (pepper)**, sliced

200 g (7 oz) **broccoli**, cut into florets

115 g (4 oz) **fresh baby corn**, cut in half diagonally

300 g (10 1/2 oz) **Chinese cabbage (wong bok)**, cut into 2.5 cm (1 inch) pieces

100 g (3 1/2 oz) **snowpeas (mangetout)**, topped and tailed

2 tablespoons **oyster sauce**

2 teaspoons **soy sauce**

1 teaspoon **sugar**

1/4 teaspoon **sesame oil**

2 teaspoons **cornflour (cornstarch)** mixed with 1 tablespoon water,
   to thicken (optional)

Heat the oil in a wok over high heat, add the garlic and ginger and cook until aromatic. Add the carrot and capsicum and stir-fry for 1 minute, then add the broccoli and toss for 1–2 minutes. Add the baby corn and cabbage and stir-fry until the cabbage starts to wilt and soften (this will take about 1 1/2 minutes). Toss in the snowpeas and cook for another minute. By this time the vegetables should have a glossy sheen and be partially cooked, with a slight crunch in them.

Reduce the heat and add the oyster sauce, soy sauce, sugar and the sesame oil. Toss well to coat. Add the cornflour mixture to thicken slightly if you wish. Serve hot with steamed rice or noodles.

water spinach in flames

serves 4 as a side dish

2 tablespoons **yellow bean sauce (taucheo)**

1 tablespoon **fish sauce**

2 tablespoons **oil**

500 g (1 lb 2 oz) **water spinach (ong choy)**,
   cut into 3 cm (1¼ inch) lengths

3 **garlic cloves**, crushed

4 **red Asian shallots**, finely sliced

Combine the yellow bean sauce and fish sauce in a small bowl.

Heat a wok over high heat, add the oil and swirl to coat. Stir-fry the water spinach for 1 minute, or until slightly wilted. Add the garlic and shallots and cook for about 15 seconds, then stir in the sauce and toss for 30 seconds, or until the leaves are well coated and the stems are tender. Serve immediately.

chinese broccoli and sesame stir-fry

serves 4 as a side dish

1 tablespoon **vegetable** or **peanut oil**

3 **garlic cloves,** crushed

1.5 kg (3 lb 5 oz/2 bunches) **Chinese broccoli (gai lan),** cut into thirds

2 teaspoons **sesame oil**

3 tablespoons **oyster sauce**

2 tablespoons toasted **sesame seeds**

Heat a wok over high heat, add the oil and swirl to coat. Cook the garlic for about 30 seconds. Add the Chinese broccoli and 2 tablespoons of water and stir-fry for 3–4 minutes, or until the broccoli has wilted and the water has evaporated.

Add the sesame oil and oyster sauce and stir-fry for 1 minute, or until coated. Serve sprinkled with sesame seeds.

capsicum, snowpea and hokkien noodle stir-fry

serves 4 as a side dish

500 g (1 lb 2 oz) **hokkien (egg) noodles**

1 tablespoon **vegetable** or **peanut oil**

1 **red onion**, cut into thin wedges

2 **garlic cloves**, crushed

3 cm (1¼ inch) piece fresh **ginger**, julienned

150 g (5½ oz) **snowpeas (mangetout)**, topped and tailed,
    large ones halved on the diagonal

1 **carrot**, halved lengthways, sliced on the diagonal

1 **red capsicum (pepper)**, julienned

4 tablespoons **Chinese barbecue sauce (char sui sauce)**

1 handful **coriander (cilantro) leaves**

Soak the noodles in boiling water for 5 minutes to soften and separate. Drain well.

Heat a wok over high heat, add the oil and swirl to coat. Add the onion, garlic and ginger and stir-fry for 1 minute. Add the snowpeas, carrot and capsicum and cook for 2–3 minutes. Stir in the noodles and barbecue sauce and cook for a further 2 minutes. Toss in the coriander leaves and serve.

biryani-style rice

serves 4 as a side dish

200 g (7 oz/1 cup) **basmati rice**

pinch of **saffron threads**

1 **cinnamon stick**

4 **cardamom pods**, smashed

1 large **potato**, cut into 2 cm
  (3/4 inch) cubes

1 teaspoon **sea salt**

3 tablespoons **vegetable** or **peanut oil**

1 **eggplant (aubergine)**,
  cut into 2 cm (3/4 inch) cubes

1 **red onion**, cut into thin wedges

3 **garlic cloves**, crushed

1 tablespoon grated fresh **ginger**

1 teaspoon **dried chilli flakes**

1 teaspoon **ground cinnamon**

1 teaspoon **ground coriander**

2 teaspoons **ground cumin**

1 teaspoon **ground cardamom**

1 teaspoon **fennel seeds**, ground

155 g (5 1/2 oz/1 1/4 cups) **green beans**,
  trimmed and cut into 2 cm (3/4 inch)
  lengths, blanched

100 g (3 1/2 oz/2/3 cup) **frozen peas**,
  thawed

50 g (1 3/4 oz/1/3 cup) **currants**

1 small handful **coriander (cilantro)**
  leaves

2 tablespoons chopped toasted
  pistachio kernels

Wash the rice under cold water until it runs clear. Put the rice, saffron, cinnamon, cardamom pods, potato cubes and salt in a large saucepan. Fill with cold water to 2 cm (3/4 inch) above the rice and bring to a simmer over low heat. When the rice starts to pocket (after about 5 minutes), cover and cook for 10 minutes, or until the rice is tender. Fluff the rice with a fork and turn out onto a flat tray to cool slightly. Discard the cinnamon stick and cardamom pods.

Heat a wok over high heat, add 2 tablespoons of the oil and swirl to coat. Add the eggplant and stir-fry for 3–4 minutes, or until softened and golden. Remove from the wok.

Heat the remaining oil in the wok, add the onion and cook for 1 minute, or until softened. Add the garlic, ginger, chilli, spices and beans and cook for 1 minute. Stir in the rice mixture, eggplant, peas, currants and coriander leaves and gently toss until combined. Serve sprinkled with the pistachios.

bacon, leek and potato stir-fry

serves 4 as a side dish

vegetable or **peanut oil**, for frying

2 **eggs**, lightly beaten

2 **bacon slices**, thinly sliced

2 **potatoes**, peeled and thinly julienned

1 **leek**, thinly julienned

2 **spring onions (scallions)**, sliced

2 tablespoons **oyster sauce**

2 teaspoons **light soy sauce**

1 teaspoon **sugar**

Heat 2 tablespoons of oil in a wok over medium heat. Swirl the egg around to form a thin omelette. As it sets flip it over to brown the other side briefly, remove from the wok, then roll up and thinly slice. Set aside.

Heat a little extra oil in the wok, add the bacon and stir-fry until golden. Remove from the wok.

Add a little more oil and stir-fry the potato over high heat for 5–6 minutes, or until just cooked and softened. Add the leek and cook for 1 minute. Return the bacon to the wok, then stir in the spring onion, oyster sauce, soy sauce and sugar. Stir-fry for 1 minute, then serve immediately, garnished with the omelette strips.

white miso and eggplant noodles

serves 4 as a side dish

1 tablespoon **white miso**

3 tablespoons **Japanese soy sauce**

1 tablespoon **mirin**

2 tablespoons **sugar**

1 teaspoon **dashi granules** (see tip)

18 g packet **dried wakame** (see tip)

600 g (1 lb 5 oz) **udon noodles**

2 tablespoons **vegetable** or **peanut oil**

2 **slender eggplants (aubergines)**, sliced on the diagonal

6 **spring onions (scallions)**, finely sliced on the diagonal

3 cm (1¼ inch) piece fresh **ginger**, julienned

150 g (5½ oz) fresh **shiitake mushrooms**, halved

1 tablespoon toasted **sesame seeds**

2 **spring onions (scallions)**, extra, finely sliced on the diagonal

Combine the miso, soy sauce, mirin, sugar and dashi in a small bowl. Put the wakame in a bowl of cold water and leave for 3 minutes to soften, then drain straight away. Put the noodles in a bowl of boiling water and leave for 5 minutes to soften and separate. Drain.

Heat a wok over high heat, add the oil and swirl to coat. Stir-fry the eggplant for 2–3 minutes, or until golden and softened. Add the spring onion, ginger and mushrooms and stir-fry for 2 minutes. Add the noodles and miso mixture and toss until well combined. Stir in the wakame and toasted sesame seeds and serve immediately, sprinkled with the extra spring onion.

tips Dashi is made from dried fish and dried kelp and is used regularly in Japanese cooking. Wakame is dried seaweed with a mild flavour and soft texture (after soaking), which increases to 10 times its volume once soaked. Both ingredients are available from Japanese supermarkets and some general supermarkets.

vegetable stir-fry with chilli jam

serves 4 as a side dish

1 tablespoon **vegetable** or **peanut oil**

1 **red onion**, cut into thin wedges

2 **garlic cloves**, crushed

1 tablespoon **chilli jam**

150 g (5½ oz) **snowpeas (mangetout)**, topped and tailed,
   halved on the diagonal

200 g (7 oz) small **broccoli florets**

150 g (5½ oz) **oyster mushrooms**, larger ones halved

1 teaspoon **sesame oil**

2 tablespoons **oyster sauce**

2 tablespoons **soy bean sauce**

1 tablespoon **Chinese rice wine**

Heat a wok over high heat, add the oil and swirl to coat. Stir-fry the red onion for 1 minute, or until softened. Add the garlic and chilli jam and cook for 30 seconds. Add the vegetables and stir-fry for a further 2 minutes.

Combine the sesame oil, oyster sauce, soy bean sauce and rice wine, add to the wok and stir-fry for about 1–2 minutes, or until the sauce has reduced slightly and coats the vegetables. Serve immediately.

sichuan rice noodles

serves 4 as a side dish

6 **dried shiitake mushrooms**

1 tablespoon **Chinese rice wine**

3 tablespoons **kecap manis**

1 tablespoon **peanut oil**

6 **spring onions (scallions)**, cut into 3 cm (1¼ inch) lengths

2 **garlic cloves**, crushed

1 teaspoon **five-spice powder**

2 tablespoons chopped **coriander (cilantro) stems and roots**

1 teaspoon **Sichuan pepper**, pounded

1 large **long red chilli**, thinly sliced on the diagonal

375 g (13 oz/1 bunch) **baby bok choy (pak choy)**, quartered lengthways

500 g (1 lb 2 oz) **fresh rice noodles** 2 cm (¾ inch) wide

1 small handful **coriander (cilantro) leaves**

2 **spring onions (scallions)**, extra, finely sliced on the diagonal

Soak the mushrooms in boiling water for 5 minutes to soften. Drain, reserving 3 tablespoons of the liquid. Discard the woody stems and finely slice the caps. Combine the reserved liquid, rice wine and kecap manis.

Heat a wok over high heat, add the oil and swirl to coat. Stir-fry the spring onion, garlic, five-spice powder, coriander stems, pepper and chilli for 1–2 minutes.

Add the bok choy, mushrooms and the mushroom sauce mixture and stir-fry for a further 2 minutes, or until the bok choy has wilted. Gently toss in the noodles until well combined and coated in the sauce. Serve sprinkled with the coriander leaves and extra spring onion.

deep-frying

why deep-fry?

There's a whole host of food that lends itself to brief cooking in very hot oil, resulting in a deliciously crisp coating and a moist, tender centre. While not necessarily something you'd do every day, deep-frying is easier than you might think. In western societies, deep-frying has acquired something of a bad reputation in recent years, but really, there's no reason not to deep-fry occasionally. It is true that a lot of oil is used in the cooking process, but when deep-frying is done properly at the correct temperature, little oil is actually absorbed into the food. Lifting the food out using a long-handled wire-mesh strainer basket (spider) drains a lot of oil, and sitting the food on crumpled paper towels immediately after cooking will also absorb much of the oil.

oil, temperature and deep-frying

The type of oil you use for deep-frying is crucial. All oils decompose when they reach a certain temperature, called the 'smoke point', but some oils reach this point sooner than others. Vegetable oils have a high smoke point (about 230°C/450°F) and are ideal for deep-frying as they don't smoke and burn the food. Peanut, vegetable or canola oil are all suitable for deep-frying. If using peanut oil, use refined peanut oil rather than cold-pressed. Not only is it cheaper, but it also has an unobtrusive flavour that is perfect for deep-frying.

While it is possible to re-use oil, it is better to use fresh for two reasons. Firstly, oil absorbs the flavours of the food that was cooked in it, particularly strongly flavoured foods such as seafood; and secondly, once oil has been heated, it turns rancid (particularly if there are food particles in it) and its structure alters. Fresh oil ensures that the flavour of the food and not the oil is predominant. If you do re-use oil, strain it before using it and don't overheat it.

In order to achieve food with a crisp exterior and a tender interior the temperature of the oil is critical. If your oil is too cold the food will take too long to cook, absorb a lot of oil and be greasy. And if the oil is too hot, the food will burn on the outside and still be undercooked inside. To ensure that the oil is the temperature required by the recipe, use a deep-frying thermometer. These are designed especially for deep-frying and either attach to the side of the wok or can be held in the oil. Alternatively, if you don't have a thermometer, use the bread test (indicated in each recipe). And remember, as with stir-frying, when food is added to the oil, the oil temperature drops, so you may need to reheat the oil before adding the next batch, or adjust the temperature as the food is cooking.

using a wok for deep-frying

Although there is no need to have more than one wok in your kitchen for different cooking methods, an important consideration when deep-frying in a wok is stability. If you can, use a two-handled wok as it is far less likely to overbalance than a one-handled wok. If you are cooking on an electric stove, use a flat-bottomed wok and if you have a gas stove, use a wok stand to make sure the wok is secure.

Never overfill the wok with oil. Between one-third and half-full is sufficient to allow room for splattering and for the oil to bubble up when the food is added. Too much oil could lead to a serious accident. Heat the oil to the required temperature and if necessary, adjust the heat when cooking to maintain it.

Ensure the ingredients are at room temperature before adding them to the oil, to minimize the drop in oil temperature and to prevent splattering. Cook the ingredients in small batches so the oil doesn't overflow.

To stop oil spitting, food should be as dry as possible. If it is coated in batter, ensure that any excess is drained off. If food has been marinated, remove it from the marinade with a slotted spoon to allow it to drain.

When deep-frying individual pieces such as fritters, gently lower them into the wok using a heatproof slotted spoon, sliding down the side of the wok.

Alternatively, put them in a spider and lower into the oil. If you are careful, you can also do this by hand.

When the food is cooking, wooden chopsticks are useful for turning food over so that it cooks evenly on both sides. They are also long enough to keep your hands away from splattering oil. You can buy very long cooking chopsticks from Asian supermarkets and some good kitchen stores. Avoid plastic chopsticks because they are harder to manipulate than bamboo.

Some people use a wire rack that sits over the side of the wok, which is useful for keeping cooked food warm while you continue to cook the rest of the food. Another method of keeping food warm, particularly if there is a lot of it, is to heat the oven to 160°C (315°F/Gas 2–3) and keep the food warm in there while you cook the rest.

Have a plate lined with crumpled paper towels ready to drain the cooked food. This is more efficient than flat paper towels as it absorbs more oil.

deep-frying techniques

An oil **thermometer** is the best way to check the oil is the **correct temperature**.

Lower food **gently down the side** of the wok to prevent the hot oil splashing.

130

Remove cooked food
with a spider to
allow excess oil to drain off.

Drain food on crumpled
paper towels
to remove excess oil.

dipping sauces

Deep-fried food can be enhanced with a dipping sauce, so pick your favourite.

Sweet cucumber dipping sauce

Put 3 tablespoons of rice vinegar in a small saucepan with 2 tablespoons of sugar and a pinch of salt. Bring slowly to the boil to dissolve the sugar. Leave to cool, then stir in a 5 cm (2 inch) piece of cucumber, diced, a 5 cm (2 inch) piece of carrot, diced, and 1 tablespoon of finely chopped coriander (cilantro) leaves. Transfer to a serving dish.

Peanut sauce

Take an unshaken 400 ml (14 fl oz) tin of coconut milk and scoop off the thick part that forms at the top (if there is none, just use about 3 tablespoons of coconut milk). Put it in a frying pan over medium heat. Add 2½ tablespoons of red curry paste and 1 tablespoon of tomato paste (purée) and stir-fry for 2 minutes, or until aromatic. Add the remaining coconut milk, 2 tablespoons of peanut butter and 70 g (2½ oz/½ cup) of ground peanuts. Simmer gently over low heat, stirring, for 3 minutes. Leave to cool before serving.

Rice vinegar and chilli dipping sauce

Put 100 ml (3½ fl oz) of rice vinegar in a small saucepan. Add 3 tablespoons of sugar and a good pinch of salt. Bring slowly to the boil to dissolve the sugar. Leave to cool slightly, then stir in 1 seeded and sliced small red chilli and 1 seeded and sliced small green chilli. Transfer to a serving dish and leave to cool completely before serving.

Creamy chilli sauce

Put 160 g (5¾ oz/⅔ cup) of sour cream in a bowl, add 3 tablespoons of sweet chilli sauce and mix together. Stir in 2 finely chopped spring onions (scallions), 2 tablespoons of chopped coriander (cilantro) and 1 tablespoon of lime juice. Mix well, then transfer to a serving dish. Chill before serving.

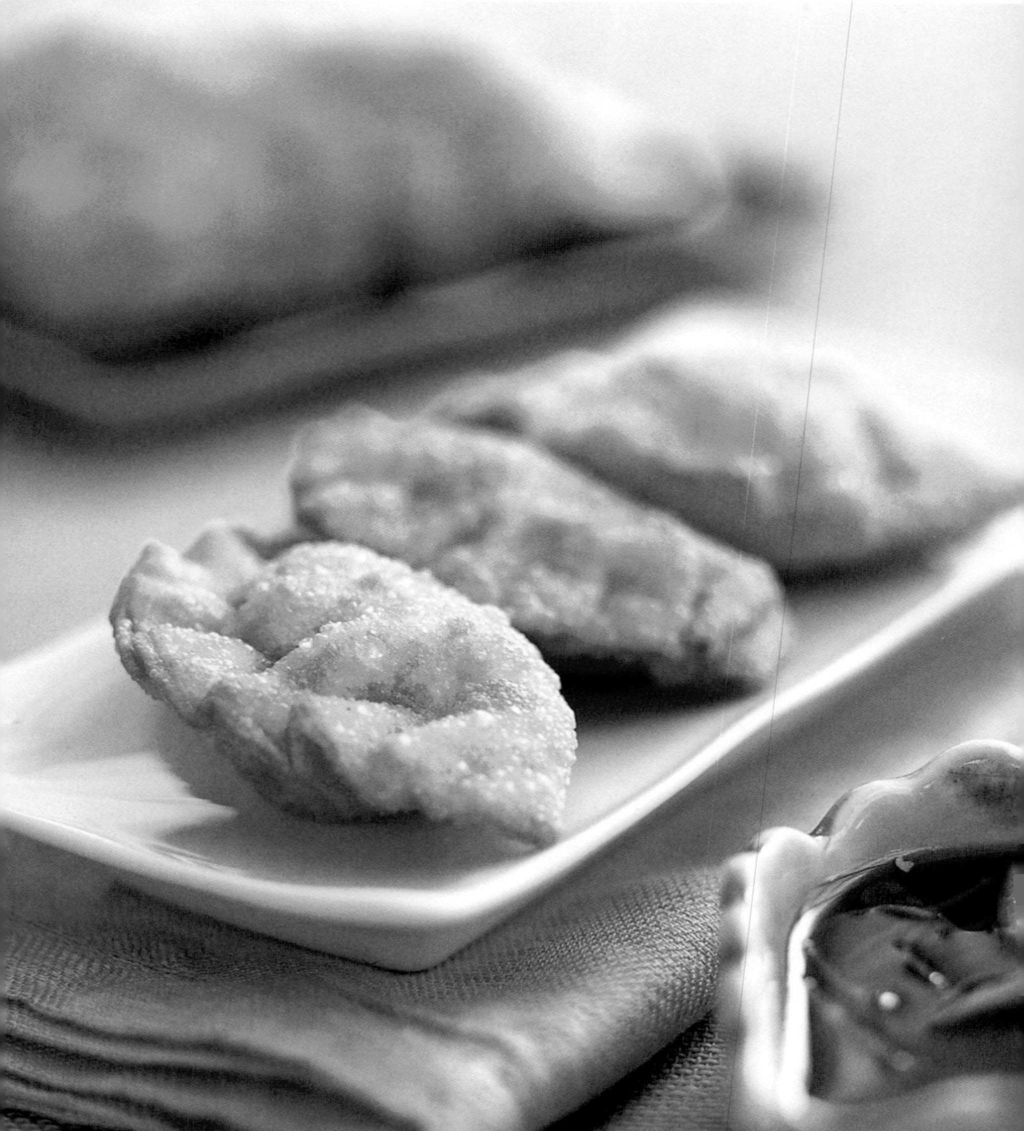

pork and prawn gow gees

makes 30

200 g (7 oz) **raw prawn (shrimp) meat**

200 g (7 oz) **minced (ground) pork**

5 **spring onions (scallions)**, chopped

2 **garlic cloves,** crushed

1 1/2 teaspoons grated fresh **ginger**

1 teaspoon **sesame oil**

1 1/2 tablespoons **soy sauce**

1 tablespoon **Chinese rice wine**

30 **gow gee wrappers**

oil, for deep-frying

dipping sauce

3 tablespoons **soy sauce**

1 tablespoon **Chinese rice wine**

3 cm (1 1/4 inch) piece fresh **ginger,**
   julienned

To make the dipping sauce, combine all the ingredients in a small bowl.

Put the prawn meat, pork, spring onion, garlic, ginger, sesame oil, soy sauce and rice wine in a food processor and blend until combined.

Put a heaped teaspoon of the mixture in the centre of each gow gee wrapper. Lightly brush the edges with a little water and fold over to form a half-moon shape. Press the edges together and fold to form small pleats.

Fill a wok one-third full of oil and heat to 180°C (350°F), or until a cube of bread dropped in the oil browns in 15 seconds. Add the gow gees in four batches and deep-fry for 2–3 minutes, or until golden and cooked through. Drain on crumpled paper towels. Serve hot with the dipping sauce.

salt and pepper squid

serves 4 as a starter

450 g (1 lb) whole **squid** or 250 g (9 oz) **squid tubes**

vegetable oil, for deep-frying

10 g (1/4 oz) **dried rice vermicelli**

2 large **red Asian shallots**, sliced

potato flour or **cornflour (cornstarch)**, for coating

2 small **red chillies**, sliced

spice mix

1 teaspoon **whole black peppercorns**

1 teaspoon **Sichuan peppercorns**

2 teaspoons **sea salt flakes**

large pinch of **five-spice powder**

To prepare the squid, remove the intestines by firmly pulling on the tentacles. Pull out the clear quill, and remove the purple membrane by pulling on the flaps. Wash under running water to remove any ink and grit. Cut the tube in half lengthways. Lightly score the flesh in a criss-cross pattern, being careful not to cut all the way through, and then cut the squid roughly into 6 x 4 cm (2½ x 1½ inch) pieces. Refrigerate until ready to use.

To make the spice mix, grind the black and Sichuan peppercorns in a mortar and pestle or small food processor until the peppercorns are crushed. Add the sea salt and five-spice powder and mix well.

Fill a wok about one-third full of vegetable oil and heat to 180°C (350°F), or until a cube of bread dropped in the oil browns in 15 seconds. Break the dried vermicelli noodles up roughly and drop them into the hot oil — they will sizzle and float to the surface almost immediately. Remove from the oil, and drain on crumpled paper towels. Add the shallots to the wok and cook until golden. Drain well; they will crisp on sitting.

Coat the squid in potato flour and drop into the hot oil. Cook for 30–60 seconds, or until lightly golden and crisp. Drain on crumpled paper towels. Coat the squid with 1–2 teaspoons of the spice mix, or to taste.

To serve, arrange the squid on a bed of crispy noodles, and top with the fried shallots and chilli slices. The extra spice mix can be served alongside for those who want more, or can be stored in a jar for use next time.

Take out the **clear quill** from the inside of the squid tube.

Remove the **purple membrane** that covers the squid.

money bags

makes 20

1 **dried shiitake mushroom**

1 tablespoon **vegetable oil**

4 **red Asian shallots**, finely chopped

1 **garlic clove**, finely chopped

1 small **red chilli**, seeded and finely chopped

2 teaspoons grated fresh **ginger**

125 g (4½ oz) **minced (ground) chicken**

1 teaspoon **ground coriander**

2 tablespoons chopped **coriander (cilantro) leaves**

2 teaspoons **fish sauce**

20 x 8 cm (3¼ inch) **won ton wrappers**

20 **chives**

vegetable oil, for deep-frying

Soak the shiitake mushroom in hot water for 10 minutes. Drain. Discard the woody stem and finely slice the cap.

Heat the oil in a wok over medium heat and swirl to coat. Stir-fry the shallots, garlic, chilli and ginger until softened but not browned. Add the chicken and ground coriander and stir-fry until the meat changes colour. Stir in the coriander leaves, fish sauce and mushroom. Allow to cool.

Spread the won ton wrappers out on a board and put a heaped teaspoon of the mixture in the middle of each. Use a finger to lightly wet with water the outer circle around the meat mixture, but not to the outer edges. Gather the wrapper points up to form a pouch and press together firmly.

Wrap a chive strand twice around the top of each won ton to form a small bag. Tie the chives into a knot to hold secure and trim. Fill a wok one-third full of vegetable oil and heat to 190°C (375°F), or until a cube of bread dropped in the oil browns in 10 seconds. Deep-fry the money bags in batches for 30–60 seconds, or until crisp and golden brown. Drain on crumpled paper towels. Serve warm with a dipping sauce (see page 132).

tip This recipe can be easily doubled.

deep-fried battered shiitake mushrooms with nam prik sauce

serves 4 as a starter

125 g (4 1/2 oz/1 cup) **plain (all-purpose) flour**
1 teaspoon **salt**
3 tablespoons **coconut milk**
250 ml (9 fl oz/1 cup) **ice-cold water**
vegetable oil, for deep-frying
200 g (7 oz) small–medium fresh **shiitake mushrooms**

nam prik sauce

1 tablespoon **soy sauce**
2 tablespoons **lemon juice**
2 teaspoons **sugar**
2 **green chillies**, halved lengthways, seeded
2 **red chillies**, halved lengthways, seeded
3 **garlic cloves**, halved
3 **red Asian shallots**, halved
2 **tomatoes**, cut into 2 cm (3/4 inch) slices
1 small **eggplant (aubergine)** (about 150 g/5 1/2 oz),
   cut into 2 cm (3/4 inch) slices

The batter can still have
a few lumps.

Wrap the food in **foil**
parcels to soften
under the **grill**.

To make the batter, combine the flour, salt, coconut milk and cold water in a bowl. Don't beat it too much — it can still have a few lumps. If it seems too thick add a little more cold water. Leave for 30 minutes while making the nam prik sauce.

Preheat the grill (broiler) to high. Put the soy sauce, lemon juice and sugar in a small saucepan and heat gently for 1–2 minutes to dissolve the sugar. Remove from the heat. Wrap the chillies, garlic and shallots in a foil package and wrap the tomatoes and eggplant in a separate foil package. Put both packages under the grill for 10–15 minutes, or until the spices and vegetables begin to soften. Remove from the foil and peel the skin from the eggplant, tomatoes and chillies. Pound all the ingredients together in a mortar and pestle or small food processor. Transfer to a bowl and stir in the soy sauce mixture, mixing well. Spoon into a serving dish and set aside until needed.

Half fill a wok with oil and heat to 180°C (350°F), or until a cube of bread dropped in the oil browns in 15 seconds. Working in batches, dip the mushrooms in the batter, allowing any excess batter to drip off, and cook for 1½–2 minutes, or until crisp and golden. Take care not to overcrowd the oil. Drain on crumpled paper towels and serve immediately with the nam prik sauce.

tip If you like your sauces really hot, leave a few of the seeds in the chillies.

deep-fried chicken wrapped in pandanus leaves

serves 4 as a starter

500 g (1 lb 2 oz) **chicken thigh fillets**, cut into 3 cm (1¼ inch) cubes

2 tablespoons **coconut cream**

1–1½ tablespoons **red curry paste**

2 tablespoons chopped **coriander (cilantro) leaves**

2 **garlic cloves**, chopped

2 teaspoons **fish sauce**

1 tablespoon finely grated **palm sugar**

pandanus leaves, for wrapping

oil, for deep-frying

sweet chilli sauce, to serve

Put the chicken, coconut cream, curry paste, coriander, garlic, fish sauce and palm sugar in a bowl and mix well to dissolve the sugar. Cover with plastic wrap and marinate in the refrigerator for at least 2 hours, or preferably overnight.

Wrap each portion of chicken in a pandanus leaf. To do this, put the chicken in the middle of the leaf and tie the leaf around to enclose as if tying a knot. Cut the leaf down to shorten it and create a little parcel, then continue with the remaining pieces.

Half-fill a wok with oil and heat to 180°C (350°F), or until a cube of bread dropped in the oil browns in 15 seconds. Add the parcels in batches and cook for about 5–6 minutes, or until the chicken is cooked and the parcels feel firm. Drain well on crumpled paper towels and serve hot with sweet chilli sauce.

tip If you prefer, you can remove the chicken from the leaves before serving.

Put the chicken pieces in the middle of **the leaf**.

Tie the leaf as if tying **a knot**.

sesame-coated tuna with wasabi mayonnaise

serves 4 as a starter

wasabi mayonnaise

125 g (4¹/2 oz/¹/2 cup) **Japanese mayonnaise**

3 teaspoons **wasabi paste**

1 tablespoon **Japanese soy sauce**

2 teaspoons **rice wine vinegar**

500 g (1 lb 2 oz) fresh **tuna**, cut into 2 cm (3/4 inch) cubes

50 g (13/4 oz/¹/3 cup) **white sesame seeds**

50 g (13/4 oz/¹/3 cup) **black sesame seeds**

oil, for deep-frying

To make the wasabi mayonnaise, combine all the ingredients in a small bowl. Set aside until ready to serve.

Put the tuna in a bowl with the sesame seeds and toss to coat evenly.

Fill a wok one-third full of oil and heat to 180°C (350°F), or until a cube of bread dropped in the oil browns in 15 seconds. Deep-fry the cubes of tuna in three batches for 1–2 minutes, or until the tuna is lightly golden and still pink in the centre. Drain on crumpled paper towels. Serve with the wasabi mayonnaise.

tip Serve the tuna on a platter with toothpicks for finger food or, if you prefer to serve it as a starter, arrange the tuna on a bed of mizuna leaves and drizzle with the mayonnaise.

151

tempura prawns and vegetables

serves 4

tempura batter

60 g (2¹/4 oz/¹/2 cup) **plain (all-purpose) flour**

60 g (2¹/4 oz/¹/2 cup) **cornflour (cornstarch)**

1 teaspoon **baking powder**

¹/4 teaspoon **salt**

about 185 ml (6 fl oz/³/4 cup) **cold water,**
   mixed with 4–6 ice cubes

16 **raw king prawns (shrimp)**, peeled and deveined, tails intact

5 **asparagus spears**, trimmed and sliced in half on the diagonal

¹/2 small **orange sweet potato**, peeled and thinly sliced

1 **red capsicum (pepper)**, cut into 2 cm (³/4 inch) wedges

2 **slender eggplants (aubergines)**, thinly sliced on the diagonal

4 large fresh **shiitake mushrooms**, cut in half

vegetable oil, for deep-frying

ready-made **tempura dipping sauce**, to serve

wasabi paste, to serve

The batter should be very lumpy — don't **overmix** it.

Remove one cooked tempura **with a spider** to drain the excess oil.

You will need to make up two separate quantities of the tempura batter because it thickens on use. Use one quantity of batter first, then mix the second batch later as it is needed. The batter is best made as close as possible to cooking time, so ensure the other ingredients are prepared beforehand.

Divide the flour, cornflour, baking powder and salt between two bowls and mix well. To one bowl add enough water, with half the ice cubes, to make up a thin batter — you will need about 90 ml (3 fl oz) per batch. Mix lightly with chopsticks for about 30 seconds. The mixture should still be very lumpy with the flour not quite mixed through.

Fill a wok one-third full of oil and heat to 180°C (350°F), or until a cube of bread dropped in the oil browns in 15 seconds. Working in batches, dip the prawns and vegetables lightly into the batter and cook until lacy, crisp and golden. Remove from the wok with a spider and drain on crumpled paper towels. When the batter becomes too thick, make up the second batch and use it straight away. Continue cooking the remaining prawns and vegetables, making sure the oil stays at 180°C (350°F) to ensure a crisp batter.

Serve on a large platter with some tempura dipping sauce and wasabi paste.

prawn toasts

makes 12

250 g (9 oz) **prawn (shrimp) meat**

2 **spring onions (scallions)**, finely chopped

2 **garlic cloves**, crushed

1 stem **lemon grass**, white part only, finely chopped

1 large handful **coriander (cilantro) leaves**, chopped

1 **egg**, lightly beaten

2 teaspoons **fish sauce**

6 slices day-old sliced **white bread**, crusts removed

vegetable oil, for deep-frying

12 **coriander (cilantro) leaves**, extra

Process the prawns in a food processor until finely chopped. Transfer to a bowl, add the spring onion, garlic, lemon grass and coriander and mix well. Stir in the egg and fish sauce to form a paste. Cover and refrigerate for at least 30 minutes.

Spread the paste evenly and thickly over the bread. Cut the bread in half into rectangles or triangles.

Fill a wok one-third full of oil and heat to 180°C (350°F), or until a cube of bread dropped in the oil browns in 15 seconds. Add a few bread slices at a time, paste-side-down, and cook for 1–2 minutes. Turn over and cook for a further minute, or until golden. Drain on crumpled paper towels. Garnish each toast with a coriander leaf and serve warm.

pakoras

makes 20

yoghurt mint dip

250 g (9 oz/1 cup) thick **plain yoghurt**

2 teaspoons **ground cumin**

2 teaspoons **honey**

3 tablespoons chopped **mint leaves**

besan batter

120 g (41/2 oz) **besan (chickpea) flour**

85 g (3 oz/2/3 cup) **self-raising flour**

11/2 teaspoons **ground coriander**

1 teaspoon **chilli powder**

1 teaspoon **garam masala**

1 teaspoon **ground cumin**

1 **garlic clove**, crushed

1 **potato**, peeled and diced

125 g (41/2 oz) **cauliflower**, cut into
small florets

125 g (41/2 oz) **broccoli**, cut into
small florets

125 g **slender eggplants (aubergines)**,
cut into small dice

80 g (23/4 oz/1/2 cup) **frozen peas**,
thawed

vegetable oil, for deep-frying

To make the yoghurt mint dip, combine all the ingredients in a small bowl.

To make the besan batter, sift the flours and spices into a large bowl. Make a well in the centre, then gradually whisk in 310 ml (11 fl oz/11/4 cups) of water together with the garlic. Season with salt. Set aside while preparing the vegetables.

Par-boil the potato in boiling water for 3 minutes, or until half cooked. Drain and cool. Mix the potato, cauliflower, broccoli, eggplant and peas into the batter.

Fill a wok one-third full of oil and heat to 180°C (350°F), or until a cube of bread dropped in the oil browns in 15 seconds. Drop a few heaped tablespoons of the batter mixture into the oil at a time, and cook until the pakoras are golden brown. Drain on crumpled paper towels. Serve hot with the yoghurt mint dip.

vegetarian spring rolls

makes 24

5 **dried shiitake mushrooms**

50 g (1¾ oz) **dried bean vermicelli noodles**

2 tablespoons **peanut oil**

2 **garlic cloves**, chopped

1 large **carrot**, cut into 5 cm (2 inch) long julienne strips

90 g (3¼ oz/1 cup) **bean sprouts**, tails trimmed

2 **spring onions (scallions)**, sliced on the diagonal

1½ tablespoons **oyster sauce**

2 teaspoons **soy sauce**

1 teaspoon **sugar**

1 tablespoon **cornflour (cornstarch)**

24 **mini spring roll wrappers** (12.5 x 12.5 cm/5 x 5 inches)

oil, for deep-frying

sweet chilli sauce, **soy sauce** or **your choice of dipping sauce**

(see page 132), to serve

Soak the shiitake mushrooms in hot water for about 10 minutes. Drain. Discard the woody stems and thinly slice the caps. In a separate bowl, soak the noodles in warm water for 10 minutes. Drain and cut into shorter segments.

Heat the peanut oil in a wok over medium heat, add the garlic and toss until aromatic. Add the carrot and stir-fry for 1–2 minutes. Add the noodles, shiitake mushrooms, bean sprouts and spring onion, toss for another minute, then stir in the oyster sauce, soy sauce and sugar. Remove from the heat and allow to cool.

Make a paste by adding 2 tablespoons of boiling water to the cornflour. Mix well.

Put one spring roll wrapper on a board with a corner pointing towards you. Put 1 tablespoon of filling in the centre and firmly roll, tucking in the sides. As you near the final corner, dab with a little of the cornflour paste to enclose the filling. Repeat to make 24 spring rolls. Cover the remaining wrappers and completed spring rolls with a damp tea towel to prevent them drying out.

Fill a wok one-third full of oil and heat to 190°C (375°F), or until a cube of bread dropped in the oil browns in 10 seconds. Add the spring rolls in batches and cook for 30–60 seconds, or until crisp and golden brown. Drain on crumpled paper towels. Serve hot with your choice of dipping sauce.

**Stir-fry the
vegetables** together

to make the filling.

Enclose the filling **firmly**

so the spring rolls don't

burst on cooking.

deep-frying

noodle cakes topped with chinese barbecue duck

makes 16

100 ml (3¹/2 fl oz) **soy sauce**

2 tablespoons **soft brown sugar**

3 tablespoons **mirin**

1 **Chinese barbecue duck**

375 g (13 oz) **dried rice stick noodles**
   (5 mm/¹/4 inch wide)

1 **egg**, lightly beaten

2 tablespoons **potato flour** or
   cornflour (cornstarch)

1 teaspoon **sesame oil**

2 tablespoons **sesame seeds**

extra **potato flour** or **cornflour**
   (cornstarch), for dusting

oil, for deep-frying

2 **spring onions (scallions)**, finely
   sliced on the diagonal

Put the soy sauce, sugar and mirin in a small saucepan and stir over low heat until the sugar dissolves. Increase the heat to high and boil for 3–4 minutes, or until thickened and syrupy.

Remove the legs and wings from the duck. Carefully ease the skin and meat away from the body, discarding any excess fat. Cut into 1 cm (¹/2 inch) thick strips.

Put the noodles in a saucepan of boiling water and cook for 2–3 minutes, or until tender. Drain and rinse under cold running water. Drain again and put them on paper towels to absorb any excess water. Cut into 8 cm (3¹/4 inch) lengths.

Combine the noodles with the egg, flour, sesame oil and sesame seeds and toss to coat. Divide the mixture into 16. Coat your palms in potato flour and press each portion very firmly between the palms of your hands to form a compressed flat patty about 6 cm (2¹/2 inches) in diameter. Turn them over to keep them compacted and in shape. Refrigerate until needed.

Fill a wok one-third full of oil and heat to 180°C (350°F), or until a cube of bread dropped in the oil browns in 15 seconds. Deep-fry the noodles in batches for 3 minutes, or until golden and crisp. Drain on crumpled paper towels. Deep-fry the duck pieces for 30 seconds to crisp up the skin, and drain on crumpled paper towels. Arrange the duck on the noodle cakes, drizzle with the soy glaze and garnish with the spring onion.

sugar cane prawns

makes 8

dipping sauce

4 tablespoons **fish sauce**

1 small **red chilli**, sliced

1 tablespoon toasted **peanuts**, finely chopped

2 teaspoons **sugar**

1 teaspoon chopped **coriander (cilantro) leaves**

650 g (1 lb 7 oz) **raw king prawns (shrimp)**, peeled and deveined

1 **egg white**

2 tablespoons **coriander (cilantro) leaves**, chopped

1 **spring onion (scallion)**, finely chopped

2 **garlic cloves**, chopped

2 teaspoons **fish sauce**

8 pieces of **sugar cane**, about 10 cm (4 inches) long and about 1–2 cm (1/2–3/4 inch) wide (see tip)

oil, for deep-frying

To make the dipping sauce, combine the fish sauce, chilli, chopped peanuts, sugar, coriander and 1 tablespoon of water in small bowl. Mix to dissolve the sugar, then set aside until ready to serve.

Put the prawns in a food processor and process until well chopped. Add the egg white and mix well. Transfer the mixture to a bowl and add the coriander, spring onion, garlic and fish sauce.

Divide the mixture into eight and, with slightly wet hands, mould a portion around the sugar cane, covering about two-thirds of the stick. Repeat with the remaining mixture and arrange on a lined baking tray.

Fill a wok one-third full of oil and heat to 190°C (375°F), or until a cube of bread dropped in the oil browns in 10 seconds. Add the sugar cane prawns in batches and cook for 4–5 minutes, or until they are golden brown and slightly puffed, turning once during cooking. Drain on crumpled paper towels and serve hot with the dipping sauce.

tip To get the most out of these, bite off some prawn, then suck on the sweet sugar cane. Tinned sugar cane is available from Asian food stores. Cut them into half thicknesses, then chop to 10 cm (4 inch) lengths.

thai chicken cakes

makes 15

dipping sauce

115 g (4 oz/1/2 cup) **caster (superfine)**
   sugar

2 teaspoons **rice wine vinegar**

1 tablespoon **sweet chilli sauce**

1/2 small **Lebanese (short) cucumber**,
   seeded and diced

500 g (1 lb 2 oz) **minced (ground)**
   chicken

4 **spring onions (scallions)**, chopped

2 **garlic cloves**, chopped

2 teaspoons **green curry paste**

4 **makrut (kaffir lime) leaves**, shredded

1 very large handful **coriander**
   (cilantro) leaves

1/8 teaspoon **lime oil** (optional)

1 tablespoon **fish sauce**

3 tablespoons **coconut cream**

50 g (13/4 oz) **snake beans**, cut into
   5 mm (1/4 inch) slices

oil, for deep-frying

To make the dipping sauce, put the sugar and 125 ml (4 fl oz/1/2 cup) of water in a small saucepan and stir over low heat until the sugar has dissolved. Bring to the boil and cook for 5 minutes, or until thick and syrupy. Cool. Stir in the vinegar, sweet chilli sauce and cucumber.

Put the chicken, spring onion, garlic, curry paste, lime leaves, coriander, lime oil, fish sauce and coconut cream in a food processor and process until well combined. Fold in the beans. Using 2 tablespoons of mixture at a time, form into 15 patties.

Fill a wok one-third full of oil and heat to 180°C (350°F), or until a cube of bread dropped in the oil browns in 15 seconds. Deep-fry the chicken cakes in three batches for 2–3 minutes, or until lightly golden and cooked through. Drain on crumpled paper towels. Serve with the dipping sauce.

deep-fried squid with ginger and shallots

serves 4 as a side dish

500 g (1 lb 2 oz) cleaned **squid tubes**

1 teaspoon **five-spice powder**

2 teaspoons **salt**

1 1/2 teaspoons **sugar**

3 **garlic cloves**, crushed

3 tablespoons **lime juice**

3 tablespoons **light soy sauce**

3 teaspoons **sesame oil**

peanut or **vegetable oil**, for deep-frying

20 g (3/4 oz) fresh **ginger**, cut into julienne strips

2 **red Asian shallots**, finely sliced

1–2 **red chillies**, chopped

1 **lime**, quartered

Cut the squid down one side to open it out, and dry with paper towels. Using a sharp knife, score into a tight diamond pattern. Combine the five-spice powder, salt, sugar, garlic, lime juice, light soy sauce and sesame oil in a small saucepan, but don't heat it yet. Brush some of the mixture over the scored side of the squid and leave to marinate for 45 minutes. Put the squid scored-side-up on a flat surface and cut into bite-sized strips.

Fill a wok one-third full of oil and heat to 180°C (350°F), or until a cube of bread dropped in the oil browns in 15 seconds. Add the squid in batches and deep-fry for 50–60 seconds, or until golden brown. Drain on crumpled paper towels, then transfer to a serving bowl.

Add the ginger, shallots and chilli to the mixture in the saucepan and stir over medium heat for 1–2 minutes, or until fragrant. Spoon over the squid and serve at once with the lime wedges. Squeeze the juice over the squid just before eating.

deep-fried prawns in batter with lemon and ginger dipping sauce

makes 24

55 g (2 oz/1/2 cup) **besan (chickpea) flour**

60 g (21/4 oz/1/2 cup) **self-raising flour**

1 teaspoon grated fresh **ginger**

1 **garlic clove**, crushed

1/2 teaspoon ground **turmeric**

lemon and ginger dipping sauce

4 tablespoons **lemon juice**

2 tablespoons grated **palm sugar**

1 tablespoon **fish sauce**

2 teaspoons grated fresh **ginger**

1 **garlic clove**, crushed

24 **raw prawns (shrimp)**, peeled and deveined,
   tails intact

vegetable oil, for deep-frying

Whisk the mixture together to form a **smooth batter**.

Holding the prawns by the tail, carefully **lower them** into the hot oil.

Sift the besan and self-raising flours into a bowl and make a well in the centre. Combine the ginger, garlic and turmeric with 250 ml (9 fl oz/1 cup) of water and add to the sifted flours all at once. Using a whisk, combine the ingredients to form a smooth batter. Set aside.

To make the dipping sauce, combine the ingredients in a bowl, stirring to dissolve the palm sugar.

Pat the prawns dry with paper towels and slit along the belly to butterfly them, being careful not to cut all the way through. Fill a wok one-third full of oil and heat to 170°C (325°F), or until a cube of bread dropped in the oil browns in 20 seconds. Holding onto the tails, dip the prawns in the batter, leaving the tails undipped. Deep-fry a few at a time until golden, then drain on crumpled paper towels. Serve warm with the dipping sauce.

prawn, corn and coriander fritters

makes 18

500 g (1 lb 2 oz) small peeled **raw prawns (shrimp)**, finely chopped

4 **spring onions (scallions)**, chopped

2 **garlic cloves**, crushed

3 tablespoons chopped **coriander (cilantro) leaves**

1 1/2 tablespoons **fish sauce**

1 **egg**, lightly beaten

30 g (1 oz/1/4 cup) **potato flour** or **cornflour**

2 x 125 g (4 1/2 oz) tins **corn kernels**, drained

oil, for deep-frying

sweet chilli sauce, to serve

Put the prawns, spring onion, garlic, coriander, fish sauce, egg and flour in a food processor and process until well combined. Fold in the corn. Using 2 tablespoons of mixture at a time, form into 18 rounds (the mixture may be very sticky). Transfer to a bowl, cover and refrigerate for 30 minutes.

Fill a wok one-third full of oil and heat to 180°C (350°F), or until a cube of bread dropped in the oil browns in 15 seconds. Deep-fry the cakes for 2 minutes, or until they are golden and cooked through. Drain on crumpled paper towels and serve with sweet chilli sauce or a dipping sauce of your choice (see page 132)

deep-fried pacific oysters with sweet thai dipping sauce

serves 4 as a side dish

24 **Pacific oysters** or any other large oyster on the shell

30 g (1 oz/¼ cup) **plain (all-purpose) flour**

1 **egg**, mixed with 3 teaspoons cold water

60 g (2¼ oz/1 cup) **panko (Japanese breadcrumbs)**
    or **dry packaged breadcrumbs**

vegetable oil, for deep-frying

sweet thai dipping sauce

4 tablespoons **white wine vinegar**

2½ tablespoons **caster (superfine) sugar**

1 slice fresh **ginger**

1 **Lebanese (short) cucumber**, seeded and finely diced

1 small **red chilli**, seeded and sliced

1 tablespoon chopped **coriander (cilantro) leaves**

Remove the oysters from their shells and lightly coat in the flour. Wash the shells, removing any grit from them, then dry well and set aside for later. Coat the oysters in the egg mixture and then the panko, pressing on firmly. Arrange the oysters on a plate, cover and refrigerate for at least 30 minutes.

To make the dipping sauce, put the vinegar, sugar and ginger in a small saucepan and heat to dissolve the sugar. Bring to the boil, then remove from the heat and allow to cool to room temperature. Discard the ginger and stir in the cucumber, chilli and coriander.

Fill a wok one-third full of oil to 180°C (350°F), or until a cube of bread dropped in the oil browns in 15 seconds. Deep-fry the oysters in batches for 1 minute, or until golden brown. Remove from the oil with a slotted spoon and drain on crumpled paper towels. Put the oysters back in the shells and drizzle with the dipping sauce or, if you prefer, serve the sauce in a bowl on the side.

deep-fried bean curd rolls

makes 8

filling

10 **dried shiitake mushrooms**

2 tablespoons **vegetable** or **peanut oil**

1 **carrot**, thinly julienned

2 **garlic cloves**, chopped

100 g (3¹/2 oz) **snowpeas (mangetout)**, topped and tailed
   and thinly sliced on the diagonal

2 tablespoons **oyster sauce**

2 teaspoons **soy sauce**

1 teaspoon **sugar**

1 teaspoon **sesame oil**

200 g (7 oz) **dried bean curd sheets** (see tip)

1 tablespoon **cornflour (cornstarch)**

vegetable oil, for deep-frying

your choice of dipping sauce (see page 132), to serve

To make the filling, soak the shiitake mushrooms in hot water for 10 minutes. Drain. Discard the woody stems and slice the caps.

Heat the oil in a wok over medium–high heat and stir-fry the carrot for 1 minute, or until softened slightly. Add the garlic, mushrooms and snowpeas, then stir in the oyster sauce, soy sauce, sugar and sesame oil until heated through. Remove from the heat. Cool to room temperature.

Trim the bean curd sheets to eight rectangles about 15 x 20 cm (6 x 8 inches), put them on a large tray and cover with cold water. Leave to soak for a few minutes, until softened, then remove carefully from the water and put on a clean dry tea towel. Pat dry slightly.

Divide the filling into eight portions. Mix the cornflour with 2½ tablespoons of water to form a paste. Take one bean curd wrapper and put a portion of filling in the centre. Roll up firmly, folding in the ends. Dab some cornflour paste on the ends to enclose. Repeat with the remaining sheets and filling.

Half-fill a wok with oil and heat to 190°C (375°F), or until a cube of bread dropped in the oil browns in 10 seconds. Add the rolls a few at a time and deep-fry for 3–4 minutes, or until golden and crisp, turning over halfway through. Serve hot, either whole or sliced in half on the diagonal, with your choice of dipping sauce.

tip Bean curd sheets are very delicate and need care and patience to work with. Buy the most pliable ones you can find. You may want to buy an extra packet as some may break or tear.

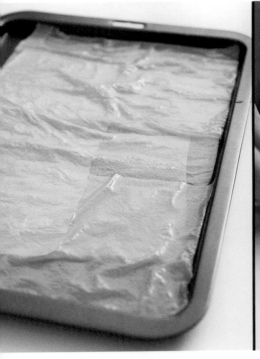

You need to soak the **bean curd sheets** before using them.

Handle the sheets carefully as they are very **delicate**.

curry puffs

makes 25

1 tablespoon **vegetable oil**

4 **spring onions (scallions)**, finely chopped

4 **coriander (cilantro) roots**, washed and finely chopped

1 **garlic clove**, finely chopped

1 teaspoon **ground turmeric**

1 teaspoon **ground coriander**

1 teaspoon **curry powder**

300 g (10½ oz) **minced (ground) pork**

1 tablespoon **fish sauce**

2 teaspoons shaved **palm sugar**

230 g (8½ oz/1 cup) **mashed potato** (see tip)

65 g (2¼ oz/½ cup) frozen **baby peas**, thawed

5 sheets **ready-rolled puff pastry**

vegetable oil, for deep-frying

sweet chilli sauce or **your choice of dipping sauce** (see page 132), to serve

Heat the oil in a wok and swirl to coat. Add the spring onion, coriander root and garlic and stir-fry over medium heat for 1 minute, or until softened but not browned. Stir in the turmeric, ground coriander and curry powder, then add the pork and stir-fry for 3–4 minutes, or until the meat changes colour. Add the fish sauce and palm sugar, and stir until the sugar has dissolved. Stir in the mashed potato and peas, mix well, then leave the mixture to cool.

Using an 8 cm (3¼ inch) cutter, cut five rounds from each pastry sheet. Put a tablespoon of the filling in the centre of each round, then fold them over and pinch the edges together to seal.

Fill a wok one-third full of oil and heat to 180°C (350°F), or until a cube of bread dropped in the oil browns in 15 seconds. Deep-fry the curry puffs in batches until crisp and golden brown. Drain on crumpled paper towels. Serve warm with your choice of dipping sauce.

tip You will need about 275 g (9¾ oz) of uncooked potatoes to give this amount of mashed potato.

deep-fried pork and prawn won tons

makes 24

filling

120 g (4¹/₂ oz) **minced (ground) pork**

3 **raw king prawns (shrimp)**, peeled and deveined, finely sliced

4 **water chestnuts**, finely chopped

1 tablespoon **oyster sauce**

1 teaspoon **soy sauce**

1/2 teaspoon **sesame oil**

1 **French** or **red Asian shallot**, finely sliced

2 teaspoons **cornflour (cornstarch)**

24 **won ton wrappers**

vegetable oil, for deep-frying

sweet chilli sauce, to serve

To make the filling, combine all the ingredients in a bowl and mix well. Cover and refrigerate until ready to use. If you can, make the filling a day in advance to give the flavours time to develop.

Put a heaped teaspoon of filling in the centre of each won ton wrapper and lightly brush the edges with water. Fold the wrapper over to enclose the filling and form a triangle.

Fill a wok one-third full of oil and heat to 190°C (375°F), or until a cube of bread dropped in the oil browns in 10 seconds. Add the won tons in batches and cook for 1–2 minutes, or until they are golden and crisp and the filling is cooked. Drain on crumpled paper towels and serve hot with sweet chilli sauce for dipping.

shanghai-style five-willow fish

serves 4

3–4 **dried Chinese mushrooms**

650 g (1 lb 7 oz) **whole carp** or **grey mullet,**
    gutted, with head and tail intact

1 teaspoon **salt**

oil, for deep-frying, plus 2 tablespoons extra

1 tablespoon julienned fresh **ginger**

2 tablespoons julienned **spring onions (scallions)**

1/2 small **carrot,** julienned

1/2 small **green capsicum (pepper),** julienned

1/2 **celery stalk,** julienned

2 **red chillies,** seeded and julienned

2 tablespoons **light soy sauce**

3 tablespoons **sugar**

3 tablespoons **rice vinegar**

1 tablespoon **Chinese rice wine**

125 ml (4 fl oz/1/2 cup) **chicken stock**

1 tablespoon **cornflour (cornstarch)**

1/2 teaspoon **roasted sesame oil**

Cutting slits in the fish helps **the heat** penetrate and cook the fish **evenly**.

Spoon **the hot oil** over the fish while it is cooking.

Soak the mushrooms in hot water for 20 minutes, then drain and squeeze out any excess water. Remove and discard the stems. Finely shred the caps.

Clean and dry the fish well. Diagonally score both sides of the fish, cutting through as far as the bone at intervals of about 2 cm (3/4 inch) — this will help the heat penetrate and allow the fish to cook. Rub the fish with the salt, inside and out.

Fill a wok one-third full of oil and heat to 190°C (375°F), or until a cube of bread dropped in the oil browns in 10 seconds. Using tongs, carefully lower the fish into the oil, belly-side-down, curling the fish to fit the curves of the wok. Cook for 6–8 minutes, spooning oil over the top of the fish. Remove from the wok and drain on crumpled paper towels, then put the fish on a long serving dish and keep warm in a low oven.

Remove the oil and wipe out the wok. Heat the wok over high heat, add the extra oil and heat until very hot. Stir-fry the mushrooms, ginger, spring onion, carrot, capsicum, celery and chilli for 1 1/2 minutes. Add the soy sauce, sugar, rice vinegar, rice wine and stock, and bring to the boil. Mix the cornflour with enough water to make a paste. Add the cornflour paste to the sauce and simmer until the sauce thickens. Sprinkle with the sesame oil and blend well. Spoon the sauce over the fish and serve immediately.

tip This recipe is a variation of the classic 'sweet and sour fish' from the Yangtze River delta, a region characterized by its delicate fish and rice dishes and for its use of tender vegetables. The 'five-willow' refers to the five julienned vegetables used for the sauce.

caramel pork

serves 4

110 g (3³/4 oz/¹/2 cup) **sugar**

oil, for deep-frying

4 large **red Asian shallots**, very finely sliced

750 g (1 lb 10 oz) **pork fillets**, trimmed and cut into 2 cm (³/4 inch) cubes

1 **egg white**, beaten until frothy

125 g (4¹/2 oz/1 cup) **potato flour** or **cornflour (cornstarch)**

5 **spring onions (scallions)**, thinly sliced on the diagonal

3 **garlic cloves**, crushed

3 cm (1¹/4 inch) piece fresh **ginger**, julienned

1 tablespoon **soy sauce**

1 tablespoon **lime juice**

3 teaspoons grated **palm sugar**

Put the sugar and 125 ml (4 fl oz/¹/2 cup) of water in a saucepan and stir over low heat until the sugar has dissolved. Bring to the boil and cook for 5 minutes, or until thickened and syrupy. Carefully stir in 150 ml (5 fl oz) of water until combined. Return to the heat and simmer for 10 minutes, or until the sauce is thick and golden.

Fill a wok one-third full of oil and heat to 180°C (350°F), or until a cube of bread dropped in the oil browns in 15 seconds. Deep-fry the shallots for about 1 minute, or until golden. Drain on crumpled paper towels.

Toss the pork in the egg white and then in the flour, shaking off any excess. Add to the wok in batches and deep-fry for 2 minutes, or until golden and cooked through. Drain on crumpled paper towels. Remove all but 1 tablespoon of oil from the wok and cook the spring onion, garlic and ginger for 1 minute. Add the caramel sauce, soy sauce, lime juice and palm sugar and stir until combined. Add the pork and toss until well coated in the sauce. Serve sprinkled with the fried shallots.

marinated stuffed chicken wings

serves 4

8 large **chicken wings**

potato flour or **cornflour (cornstarch)**,
   for coating

vegetable oil, for deep-frying

2 **spring onions (scallions)**, sliced
   on the diagonal

marinade

1 1/2 tablespoons **light soy sauce**

1 tablespoon **honey**

2 teaspoons grated fresh **ginger**

2 **garlic cloves**, finely chopped

filling

180 g (6 oz) **minced (ground) pork**

60 g (2 1/4 oz/1/3 cup) chopped **water
   chestnuts**

2 tablespoons chopped **coriander
   (cilantro) leaves**

2 teaspoons **cornflour (cornstarch)**

3 teaspoons grated fresh **ginger**

2 **garlic cloves**, chopped

2 teaspoons **oyster sauce**

2 teaspoons **light soy sauce**

1/4 teaspoon **sesame oil**

Prepare the chicken by cutting down the middle through the loose skin, slightly closer to the drumstick. Twist and break the joint between one small drumstick and the wing, then cut through the joint. Take the wing section and, using a small sharp knife, gently scrape the meat away from the bone, being careful not to break the skin. Pull the bone away and discard. Carefully remove the bone from the small drumsticks by scraping the meat away from the bone. Put all the chicken pieces in a large bowl.

To make the marinade, combine all the ingredients in a bowl. Add the chicken and mix well. Cover and leave to marinate for at least 1 hour, or preferably overnight.

To make the filling, combine all the ingredients. Gently spoon into the deboned wings and drumsticks, and lightly coat in potato flour. Half-fill a wok with oil and heat to 170°C (325°F), or until a cube of bread dropped in the oil browns in 20 seconds. Add the chicken in batches and cook for 8 minutes, or until cooked through. Don't have the oil too hot, otherwise you will find the chicken will brown too quickly and the centre won't cook. Drain on crumpled paper towels.

Garnish with the spring onion and serve with steamed rice and green vegetables.

mee krob

serves 4

100 g (3¹/2 oz) **dried rice vermicelli**

1 **egg white**, beaten

peanut or **vegetable oil**, for deep-frying

125 g (4¹/2 oz) **minced (ground) pork**

125 g (4¹/2 oz) **raw prawn (shrimp) meat**, chopped

1 tablespoon **vegetable oil**, extra

2 **coriander (cilantro) roots**, finely chopped

3 **garlic cloves**, crushed

2 cm (3/4 inch) piece fresh **ginger**, grated

2 tablespoons **fish sauce**

2 tablespoons **palm sugar**

1 tablespoon **chilli sauce**

2 teaspoons **grated orange zest**

1 tablespoon **lime juice**

150 g (5¹/2 oz) **bean sprouts**, tails trimmed

1/2 small **red chilli**, finely chopped

3 tablespoons torn **coriander (cilantro) leaves**

2 tablespoons snipped **garlic chives**

Put the vermicelli in a bowl, cover with warm water and soak for 10–15 minutes. Drain well and return to a dry bowl. Add the egg white and toss to coat. Spread the noodles on a tray and leave out overnight to dry — this will seal the noodles and make them crisp when fried.

Fill a wok one-third full of oil and heat to 180°C (350°F), or until a cube of bread dropped in the oil browns in 15 seconds. Add the noodles in batches and cook for 10–15 seconds, or until crisp and light golden. Drain on crumpled paper towels. Leave the oil to cool.

Pour off all but 1 tablespoon of the oil from the wok. Add the pork and cook, stirring, over high heat for about 1 minute, or until browned. Add the prawn meat and stir-fry for 60–90 seconds, or until opaque. Remove from the wok.

Add the oil, coriander root, garlic, ginger, fish sauce, palm sugar and chilli sauce. Season with a good pinch of salt and cook, stirring, over low heat for 1 minute. Stir in the orange zest, lime juice and bean sprouts and cook for 30 seconds. Return the pork and prawn mixture to the wok and cook for 30–40 seconds. Remove from the heat and add the chilli, coriander leaves, chives and crispy noodles. Toss well and serve immediately.

Deep-fry the **noodles** in batches until crisp and **lightly golden**.

Toss the food around **the wok** for quick and even cooking.

deep-fried marinated pork with green papaya salad

serves 4

3 tablespoons **kecap manis**

50 g (1³/4 oz) grated **palm sugar**

1¹/2 tablespoons **oyster sauce**

1 **star anise**

1 **makrut (kaffir lime) leaf**, shredded

250 g (9 oz) **pork neck**, cut into 2 cm
(3/4 inch) cubes

vegetable oil, for deep-frying

green papaya salad

550 g (1 lb 4 oz) **green papaya**, peeled
and coarsely grated

3 tablespoons **dried shrimp**, soaked
in hot water for 10 minutes, then
finely chopped

40 g (1¹/2 oz/¹/4 cup) toasted **unsalted
peanuts**, coarsely chopped

4 **snake beans**, cut into 4 cm (1¹/2 inch)
lengths, julienned

3 **bird's eye chillies**, seeded and
finely chopped

1 **garlic clove**, crushed

2 teaspoons **lime juice**

1 tablespoon **fish sauce**

1 teaspoon **soft brown sugar**

1 teaspoon **rice vinegar**

1 **baby Chinese cabbage (wong bok)**,
outer leaves only

Put the kecap manis, sugar, oyster sauce, star anise, lime leaf and a pinch of salt in a saucepan and simmer gently for 2–3 minutes, or until syrupy. Cool completely. Put the syrup and pork in a bowl and toss to coat. Cover and refrigerate overnight.

To make the salad, put the papaya, dried shrimp, peanuts, snake beans, chilli and garlic in a bowl. Combine the lime juice, fish sauce, brown sugar and vinegar in a small bowl, add 1¹/2 tablespoons of water and mix well. Pour over the papaya mixture and toss to coat. Arrange 2–3 cabbage leaves on each of four serving plates to hold the salad. Spoon on the salad.

Fill a wok one-third full of oil and heat to 180°C (350°F), or until a cube of bread browns in 15 seconds. Drain the pork in a sieve, shaking off the excess syrup. Add to the wok in batches and cook for 2–3 minutes, or until crisp and deep brown. Drain well. Pile the pork on top of the salad and serve hot or at room temperature.

double-fried shredded beef

serves 4

2 **eggs**, lightly beaten

40 g (1 1/2 oz/1/3 cup) **cornflour (cornstarch)**

500 g (1 lb 2 oz) **rump steak** or **beef sirloin**, cut into thin strips

vegetable oil, for deep-frying

1 **onion**, sliced

1 **carrot**, cut into thin 5 cm (2 inch) strips

2 **garlic cloves**, chopped

2 small **red chillies**, sliced

2 **spring onions (scallions)**, sliced on the diagonal

4 tablespoons **Chinese black vinegar**

80 g (2 3/4 oz/1/3 cup) **caster (superfine) sugar**

2 tablespoons **soy sauce**

2 teaspoons toasted **sesame seeds**, to garnish

Combine the beaten egg and cornflour in a bowl. Add the beef and toss to coat. Fill a wok one-third full of oil and heat to 170°C (325°F), or until a cube of bread dropped in the oil browns in 20 seconds. Using your hands and working in batches, carefully drop strips of the beef into the oil, separating them as you go. Cook for 20–30 seconds, or until the strips are golden brown. Remove with a slotted spoon and drain on crumpled paper towels.

Remove all but 2 tablespoons of the oil from the wok (or use another wok). Heat the oil over medium heat and cook the onion and carrot for about 1 minute, or until softened. Add the garlic, chilli and spring onion and stir-fry until aromatic. Add the fried beef strips, black vinegar, sugar and soy sauce and toss for 1–2 minutes, or until the sauce becomes glazy.

Sprinkle the sesame seeds over the top and serve with steamed rice.

deep-fried honey chilli chicken

serves 4

4 **chicken breast fillets**

vegetable oil, for deep-frying

plain (all-purpose) flour, for coating

3 tablespoons **honey**

2 tablespoons **chilli sauce**

4 tablespoons **lemon juice**

2 teaspoons **light soy sauce**

5 cm (2 inch) piece fresh **ginger**, thinly shredded

4 **spring onions (scallions)**, thinly shredded

2 small **zucchini (courgettes)**, thinly shredded

1 **carrot**, thinly shredded

3 **spring onions (scallions)**, extra, sliced on the diagonal

Cut each chicken breast into four pieces. Fill a large wok one-third full of oil and heat to 180°C (350°F), or until a cube of bread dropped in the oil browns in 15 seconds. Coat the chicken pieces lightly with seasoned flour, shaking off any excess. Add a few pieces of chicken at a time to the wok and cook for 3–4 minutes, or until cooked and golden brown. Drain on crumpled paper towels.

Mix together the honey, chilli sauce, lemon juice and soy sauce.

Remove all but 1 tablespoon of oil from the wok and heat. Stir-fry the ginger, spring onion, zucchini and carrot for 1 minute. Add the honey and chilli mixture, bring to the boil and cook until a little syrupy.

Return the chicken pieces to the wok and toss in the sauce and vegetables for 1–2 minutes, or until heated through. Serve on a bed of noodles or rice, garnished with the extra spring onion.

deep-fried prawn balls with asian greens

serves 4

prawn balls
350 g (12 oz) **raw prawn (shrimp) meat**, chopped
80 g (2¾ oz/1 cup) **fresh white breadcrumbs**
2 **spring onions (scallions)**, finely chopped
2 teaspoons grated fresh **ginger**
1 **egg yolk**
1 teaspoon **cornflour (cornstarch)**

vegetable oil, for deep-frying
1 tablespoon julienned fresh **ginger**

100 g (3½ oz) **snowpeas (mangetout)**, topped and tailed
100 g (3½ oz) **sugar snap peas**, trimmed
500 g (1 lb 2 oz) **baby bok choy (pak choy)**, trimmed, washed and quartered lengthways
2 tablespoons **mirin**
1 tablespoon **oyster sauce**
1 tablespoon **sweet chilli sauce**
1½ large handfuls **coriander (cilantro) leaves**

To make the prawn balls, process the prawn meat, breadcrumbs, spring onion, ginger, egg yolk and cornflour in a food processor until the mixture comes together. Using wet hands form into 12 golf ball-sized balls. Refrigerate for 20 minutes.

Fill a wok one-third full of oil and heat to 180°C (350°F), or until a cube of bread dropped in the oil browns in 15 seconds. Cook the prawn balls a few at a time for 2–3 minutes, or until cooked through and golden. Remove with a slotted spoon. Drain on crumpled paper towels.

Pour off all but 1 tablespoon of oil from the wok. Heat, then add the ginger, snowpeas and sugar snap peas and stir-fry over high heat for 2 minutes. Add 3 tablespoons of water and stir in the bok choy. Cover the wok and steam, stirring occasionally, for 3–4 minutes, or until the vegetables are just tender.

Stir in the combined mirin, oyster sauce and sweet chilli sauce. Add the prawn balls and toss well. Garnish with coriander leaves and serve with jasmine rice.

deep-fried duck breast with banana blossom

serves 4 as part of a spread

3 **duck breasts**

250 ml (9 fl oz/1 cup) cold **green tea** (can use a tea bag)

pinch of **five-spice powder**

1 **lemon**, halved

1 large **banana blossom flower** (see tip)

2 tablespoons shredded **Vietnamese mint**, plus 1 handful leaves, extra

2 tablespoons grated fresh **ginger**

2 tablespoons **crisp fried shallots**

1 large handful **coriander (cilantro) leaves**

2 **red chillies**, seeded and finely sliced

1 tablespoon coarsely chopped toasted **unsalted peanuts**

peanut or **vegetable oil**, for deep-frying

dressing

1 teaspoon **rice vinegar**

1 teaspoon **soft brown sugar**

1 tablespoon **lime juice**

2 tablespoons **fish sauce**

3 tablespoons **fresh coconut juice** or **water**

Remove the **purple** outer leaves of the banana blossom and use only the pale **inner core**.

Slice the flesh thinly, working **quickly** to prevent **discolouration**.

Put the duck breasts side by side in a saucepan and cover with cold water. Add 1 teaspoon of salt, bring to the boil, then reduce the heat and simmer for 2 minutes. Remove from the water and transfer to a bowl. Add the green tea and five-spice powder and leave to marinate for 1 hour.

Squeeze the juice from a lemon half into a large glass or ceramic bowl of very cold water. Using a stainless steel knife (to avoid discolouration) remove the leaves of the banana blossom down to its pale heart, reserving four good leaves for serving. Rub the cut surfaces with the remaining lemon half as you go. Quarter the heart from top to bottom and discard the stamens. Finely slice the flesh and immediately put it in the lemon water. Combine the shredded and whole Vietnamese mint leaves, ginger, fried shallots, coriander, chilli and peanuts in a bowl.

To make the dressing, combine all the ingredients in a small bowl.

Fill a wok one-third full of oil and heat to 180°C (350°F), or until a cube of bread dropped in the oil browns in 15 seconds. Drain the duck breasts and dry on paper towels. Add to the wok and cook until crisp and golden brown — this will take 3–5 minutes per side, depending on how rare you like your duck. Drain well on crumpled paper towels and slice diagonally.

Drain the banana blossom well and add to the salad bowl. Pour in the dressing and toss to coat. If liked, serve the duck and salad in the reserved banana blossom leaves. Alternatively, arrange the salad on individual plates, top with the sliced duck and serve.

tip Banana blossom flowers are the purple, tear-drop shaped part of the banana plant, available from Asian supermarkets. After the purple leaves and pale yellow buds are discarded, the pale inner core can be eaten. Shredded banana blossom doesn't keep for longer than 30–40 minutes, so this salad can't be prepared in advance. Shredded witlof (chicory/Belgian endive) can be used instead of the banana blossom. If so, omit the lemon-water step.

deep-fried spare ribs with chilli plum sauce

serves 4

1 tablespoon **rice vinegar**

2 tablespoons **soy sauce**

1 kg (2 lb 4 oz) **pork spare ribs**, cut into 5 cm (2 inch) pieces

3 tablespoons **plain (all-purpose) flour**

2 tablespoons **cornflour (cornstarch)**

vegetable oil, for deep-frying

2 **spring onions (scallions)**, shredded

1 **long red chilli**, seeded and shredded

chilli plum sauce

2 teaspoons **vegetable oil**

1 **garlic clove**, crushed

1 teaspoon grated fresh **ginger**

2 **spring onions (scallions)**, finely chopped

125 ml (4 fl oz/1/2 cup) **bottled plum sauce**

1 tablespoon **sweet chilli sauce**

2 teaspoons **soy sauce**

Mix the vinegar and soy sauce together in a flat dish. Add the ribs, toss until well coated then cover and refrigerate for at least 30 minutes. Drain the ribs and pat dry with paper towels. Combine the flours on a flat plate and lightly coat the ribs.

Fill a large wok one-third full of oil and heat to 180°C (350°F), or until a cube of bread dropped in the oil browns in 15 seconds. Deep-fry the ribs a few at a time until well cooked and golden brown. Drain on crumpled paper towels.

To make the chilli plum sauce, clean the wok and heat the oil. Add the garlic, ginger and spring onion and stir-fry for 1 minute. Add the plum sauce, sweet chilli sauce and soy sauce and stir to combine.

Add the ribs to the sauce and cook for 2–3 minutes, stirring until the ribs are well coated, heated through and a little sticky. Garnish with the shredded spring onion and chilli. Serve with steamed rice and vegetables.

tip The chilli plum sauce could be doubled and served as a dipping sauce.

twice-cooked chicken with black vinegar dressing

serves 4

8 **chicken pieces** (leg, breast, thigh), with bone in

1 small **onion**, quartered

1 **carrot**, quartered

5 **whole black peppercorns**

vegetable oil, for deep-frying

2 **spring onions (scallions)**, thinly sliced

black vinegar dressing

3 tablespoons **black vinegar**

4 tablespoons **vegetable oil**

1 tablespoon **soy sauce**

1 small **red chilli**, seeded and finely chopped

2 tablespoons chopped **coriander (cilantro) leaves**

Put the chicken pieces in a large saucepan with the onion, carrot and peppercorns. Pour in enough water to cover the chicken by 2.5 cm (1 inch) and bring slowly to the boil. Once boiling, reduce the heat and simmer for about 6 minutes. Remove from the heat and set aside to cool completely in the liquid (the chicken will continue to cook during this time).

To make the dressing, whisk together the vinegar, oil, soy sauce, chilli and coriander.

Remove the chicken from the cooking liquid and pat dry with paper towels. Half-fill a wok with oil and heat to 190°C (375°F), or until a cube of bread dropped in the oil browns in 10 seconds. Cook the chicken pieces for 41/2–5 minutes, or until golden and crisp. Drain well and transfer to serving plates. Pour the dressing over the chicken, scatter the spring onion over the top and leave for 5 minutes before serving. Serve with boiled rice or noodles.

deep-fried fish with chilli jam

serves 4

chilli jam

1 tablespoon **oil**

1 **red onion**, finely chopped

4 **garlic cloves**, crushed

2 tablespoons finely chopped **coriander (cilantro) roots and stems**

6 **long red chillies**, seeded and finely chopped

1 1/2 tablespoons **hoisin sauce**

1 1/2 tablespoons **fish sauce**

95 g (3 1/4 oz/ 1/2 cup) **soft brown sugar**

125 g (4 1/2 oz/1 cup) **self-raising flour**

1 teaspoon **salt**

125 ml (4 fl oz/ 1/2 cup) **chilled sparkling mineral water**

vegetable oil, for deep-frying

4 **white fish fillets** (such as perch, barramundi or snapper)

coriander (cilantro) leaves, to serve

To make the chilli jam, heat a wok over high heat, add the oil and swirl to coat. Cook the onion for 2–3 minutes. Add the garlic, coriander and chilli and cook for 1 minute. Stir in the hoisin sauce, fish sauce, sugar and 100 ml (3 1/2 fl oz) of water and cook for 8 minutes, or until reduced.

Make a batter by sifting the flour and salt into a bowl. Add the mineral water and 4 tablespoons of cold water and whisk until smooth.

Fill a wok one-third full of oil and heat to 180°C (350°F), or until a cube of bread dropped in the oil browns in 15 seconds. Dip one piece of fish at a time into the batter and deep-fry in the oil for 2–3 minutes, or until the fish is golden and cooked. Drain on crumpled paper towels. Repeat with the remaining fish and batter. Serve topped with the chilli jam and garnish with coriander.

chilli crab

serves 4

1 kg (2 lb 4 oz) fresh **blue swimmer crabs**

vegetable oil, for deep-frying

3 **garlic cloves**, crushed

2 teaspoons grated fresh **ginger**

3 small **red chillies**, finely chopped

4 **spring onions (scallions)**, finely chopped

125 ml (4 fl oz/1/2 cup) **tomato sauce (ketchup)**

3 tablespoons **chicken stock**

1/2 teaspoon **salt**

1 tablespoon **sugar**

2 tablespoons **sweet chilli sauce**

2 tablespoons **hoisin sauce**

1 tablespoon **dark soy sauce**

To prepare the crab, lift the apron (the small flap on the underside of the shell) and prise off the top hard shell. Remove any organs and the feather-like grey gills. Cut each crab into four pieces.

Fill a wok one-third full of oil and heat to 180°C (350°F), or until a cube of bread dropped in the oil browns in 15 seconds. Add the crab in batches and deep-fry for 1 minute. Drain on crumpled paper towels.

Drain all but 1 tablespoon of oil from the wok, add the garlic, ginger, chilli and spring onion and cook for 2 minutes. Combine the remaining ingredients, add to the wok and cook for 2–3 minutes, or until reduced slightly. Add the crab and toss to coat. Reduce the heat to low, then cover and cook for 3 minutes, or until the crab is cooked through. Serve with bowls of water for rinsing hands while eating.

deep-fried quail with spice sprinkle and dipping sauce

serves 4

2 tablespoons **vegetable oil**

2 teaspoons **light soy sauce**

2 teaspoons **chilli sauce**

2 teaspoons grated **palm sugar**

2 tablespoons chopped **coriander (cilantro) roots and stems**

3 teaspoons grated fresh **ginger**

3 **garlic cloves**, crushed

3 teaspoons **red curry paste**

8 **quail**

vegetable oil, for deep-frying

sprinkling mix

2 teaspoons **coriander seeds**

2 teaspoons **white peppercorns**

2 teaspoons **cumin seeds**

pinch of **mace**

1 **cardamom pod**

dipping sauce

3 tablespoons **fresh coconut juice** or **water** (see tip)

1 teaspoon grated **palm sugar**

2 teaspoons **lime juice**

1 tablespoon **fish sauce**

1 **bird's eye chilli**, seeded and thinly sliced

Combine the oil, soy sauce, chilli sauce, palm sugar, coriander, ginger, garlic and red curry paste in a large shallow bowl. Rub the marinade over both sides of each quail, then put them all in the bowl. Cover and leave to marinate overnight in the refrigerator.

To make the sprinkling mix, grind the coriander seeds, peppercorns, cumin seeds, mace and cardamom pod in a mortar and pestle or spice mill. Stop grinding while there is still some texture to the mix. Transfer to a small bowl.

To make the dipping sauce, stir the coconut juice and palm sugar together in a small bowl until the sugar dissolves. Add the lime juice, fish sauce and chilli and mix together well.

Half-fill a wok with oil and heat to 170°C (325°F), or until a cube of bread dropped in the oil browns in 20 seconds. Wipe the excess marinade off the quail and add them to the wok a few at a time. Deep-fry each batch for about 4 minutes, or until golden. Drain on crumpled paper towels and serve at once with the sprinkling mix and the dipping sauce.

tip Coconut juice is the thin liquid found within a coconut. It should not be confused with coconut milk, which is extracted from the flesh.

Use **aromatic spices** to add depth and flavour to a dish.

Grind the spices, ensuring there is still some **texture** left.

223

sesame-coated salmon with coriander relish and garlic chips

serves 4

coriander relish

2 large handfuls **coriander (cilantro) leaves**

2 tablespoons chopped **coriander (cilantro) stems**

2 **garlic cloves**, crushed

3 **spring onions (scallions)**, chopped

1 teaspoon **ground cumin**, dry-fried

1 tablespoon **desiccated coconut**

2 teaspoons **lime juice**

3 tablespoons **coconut milk**

3 teaspoons **fish sauce**

vegetable oil, for deep-frying

4 large **garlic cloves**, very finely sliced

4 **salmon fillets**, skin and all bones removed

2 **egg whites**, beaten until frothy

155 g (5½ oz/1 cup) **white sesame seeds**

To make the relish, put all the ingredients in a food processor and process until combined. Spoon into a small bowl.

Fill a wok one-third full of oil and heat to 180°C (350°F), or until a cube of bread dropped in the oil browns in 15 seconds. Deep-fry the garlic for 30 seconds, or until lightly golden and crisp. Drain on crumpled paper towels.

Coat the salmon fillets in the egg white, letting any excess drip off, then coat in the sesame seeds. Deep-fry the salmon in batches for 2 minutes, or until cooked but still pink in the centre. Drain on crumpled paper towels. Sprinkle the garlic chips over the top and serve with the coriander relish.

curries and one-pots

why use a wok?

Although most people associate woks with stir-frying, they are versatile enough to be used for curries, one-pots and soups. They are perfect for the initial spice-frying stage — a vital part of making the majority of curries — and their large surface area is excellent for the rapid evaporation and concentration of flavour for dry curries. Similarly, many Asian soups use a spice paste to provide the underlying flavour. The spices are fried in a little oil, then liquid and other ingredients are added to make the soup. Woks are perfect for these types of soups because they provide the perfect vessel for frying spices and are so close to the heat source that the flavours of the seasoning ingredients can develop rapidly.

using your wok for curries and one-pots

When using a wok for slowly cooked braises and saucy dishes, the temperature and liquid levels should be closely monitored so that the sauce doesn't evaporate too quickly and start to stick before the meat or poultry becomes tender. Make sure you check whether the recipe specifies to use a lid and at what stage it can be removed if the sauce needs to reduce and thicken.

If you're making a dry curry, keep an eye on the sauce as it evaporates to ensure that the food doesn't burn or stick to the bottom of the wok.

For quick-cooking curries, the meat is often sliced in slender strips rather than cut into large cubes; this minimizes the cooking time as they only need to be cooked long enough to just cook through and allow the sauce flavours time to develop.

perfect results for your curries

Authentic curries are made from scratch, including the toasting and grinding of whole spices. Although you can use pre-ground spices, toasting and grinding whole spices really brings out their depth of flavour. A mortar and pestle is a good way to crush the spices, but a small food processor or spice blender works equally well and is quicker.

Many recipes use home-made pastes. Although they take a little time to prepare, they generally make enough for at least two curries (the leftover paste can be frozen). A home-made paste makes all the difference.

When using tamarind to make a slowly cooked dish, it is best to use either a stainless steel or non-stick wok. The acidity of tamarind reacts badly with carbon steel woks and can strip off their much-desired seasoning layer if left in contact with the wok for long periods. Food can also be tainted.

As with many slow-cooked dishes, the flavour of curries and one-pots is enhanced by leaving them to mature, covered in the refrigerator, for up to 3 days. They can be frozen for up to 1 month. Seafood dishes are an exception to this. They do not freeze well and should be eaten on the day they are made.

cooking soup in a wok

When using a wok to cook soups, pay attention to the liquid level because it can evaporate quickly and will need to be replenished. It is also important to cover the wok with a lid, if specified in the recipe, as the evaporation created by the wok's large surface area will concentrate the flavours and result in a very strong-tasting, thick soup.

Because woks have such excellent heat conductivity, it is important to cook long-simmered soups on as low a heat as is possible, and to follow instructions for using a lid. Additional water or stock may need to be added if the liquid evaporates too rapidly.

Non-stick and stainless steel woks are best for clear or slow-cooked soups, as the long cooking time of such soups can also cause the seasoning layer to be stripped off, which will discolour the soup. When cooking soups, carbon steel woks are best suited to quickly cooked or compiled soups, or those that start by frying off a spice paste.

secrets to making soups

The flavour of soups is improved by using home-made stock. If possible, make your stock a day ahead and store it in the refrigerator. This will improve the flavours and allow any fat to be easily skimmed off. If you don't have the time to make your own, there is a wide range of commercially available stocks. In addition to those found in most supermarkets, many Asian grocery stores sell good stock in cans (it is very salty, so it might need to be diluted if you are using a lot). Some butchers and fish retailers also sell stock made on the premises, so check your local outlets.

When cooking noodle soups, soak or cook the noodles before adding them to the soup, otherwise the starches released will make the soup cloudy. Another approach is to place the noodles in the serving bowls before ladling the soup over the top.

one-pot techniques

Dry-frying whole spices is the basis to a fantastic one-pot or curry.

Fry the curry paste first so you don't end up with **raw-tasting spices** in your finished dish.

Cook meat in batches so it **seals on the outside** and is tender on the inside.

Once the spices and meat are cooked, add the liquid, such as **coconut milk** or stock.

chicken pho

serves 4 as a starter

2.5 litres (87 fl oz/10 cups) **chicken stock**

8 **black peppercorns**

2 cm (3/4 inch) piece fresh **ginger**, sliced

1 **onion**, thinly sliced

3 tablespoons **crisp fried shallots** (see tip)

1–1½ tablespoons **fish sauce**

1 **chicken breast fillet**, trimmed

500 g (1 lb 2 oz) **fresh round rice noodles**

3 tablespoons chopped **coriander (cilantro) leaves**

90 g (3¼ oz/1 cup) **bean sprouts**, tails trimmed

3 tablespoons **Vietnamese mint**

3 tablespoons **Thai basil**

2 small **red chillies**, sliced

lime wedges, to serve

Put the stock in a wok with 125 ml (4 fl oz/½ cup) of water, the peppercorns, ginger, onion, crisp fried shallots, fish sauce and ½ teaspoon of salt. Bring to the boil over high heat, then reduce the heat so the stock is just simmering and cook for 5 minutes. Put the chicken fillet in the stock and gently poach for 12–15 minutes, or until just cooked through and tender. Remove the chicken, shred and set aside. Strain the stock, then return it to a clean wok and bring to a simmer.

Put the noodles in a heatproof bowl and cover with boiling water. Gently separate them, then drain and rinse under cold water and divide among four serving bowls. Top the noodles with the shredded chicken, then ladle on the stock. Garnish with the chopped coriander, bean sprouts, mint, basil and chilli slices. Serve with lime wedges on the side.

tip Crisp fried shallots are available in jars from Asian supermarkets.

thai-style mussels in aromatic coconut sauce

serves 4 as a starter

1 kg (2 lb 4 oz) **black mussels** (about 40 mussels)

1 stem **lemon grass**, chopped into 2 cm (3/4 inch) pieces

2 **makrut (kaffir lime) leaves**, torn

1 tablespoon **vegetable oil**

1 **red onion**, finely chopped

2 **garlic cloves**, finely chopped

1 tablespoon **red curry paste**

270 ml (91/2 fl oz) tin **coconut milk**

1 tablespoon **fish sauce**

1 tablespoon **lime juice**

2 teaspoons grated **palm sugar**

1 **long red chilli**, cut into thin strips

2 **makrut (kaffir lime) leaves**, extra, shredded

Scrub the mussels clean and remove the beards. Discard any opened mussels that do not close when tapped on the work surface. Bring 750 ml (26 fl oz/3 cups) of water to the boil in a large saucepan and stir in the lemon grass and lime leaves. Add the mussels and cook, covered, for 2–3 minutes, or until the mussels have opened. Discard any unopened ones. Remove the mussels from the cooking liquid using a slotted spoon.

Meanwhile, heat the oil in a large wok. Add the onion and garlic and stir-fry for 2 minutes, or until softened. Add the curry paste and stir-fry for 1 minute, then stir in the coconut milk. Bring the sauce to the boil, then reduce the heat and simmer for 3 minutes. Add the fish sauce, lime juice and palm sugar.

Arrange the mussels in serving bowls, pour the sauce over the top and garnish with strips of chilli and shredded lime leaves.

onions with red lentils

serves 4 as a starter

3 tablespoons **ghee**

2 teaspoons **black mustard seeds**

1 **white onion**, finely chopped

1 **red onion**, halved and cut into small wedges

3 **garlic cloves**, crushed

1 teaspoon **ground turmeric**

1 teaspoon **ground cumin**

2 small **green chillies**, seeded and finely chopped

225 g (8 oz) **red lentils**

300 ml (10 1/2 fl oz) **coconut milk**

3 **spring onions (scallions)**, sliced

1 large handful **coriander (cilantro) leaves**

naan bread, to serve

lemon or **lime wedges**, to serve

Heat the ghee in a wok and add the mustard seeds. When they start to pop, add the white and red onion. Cook over medium heat for 4–5 minutes, or until just starting to brown. Stir in the garlic, cook for a further 30 seconds, then add the turmeric, cumin and chilli. Cook for 2 minutes.

Stir in the lentils, coconut milk and 1 litre (35 fl oz/4 cups) of warm water. Bring to the boil, then cover and simmer over low heat for 45–55 minutes, or until the lentils are tender and have absorbed most of the liquid. Season well with salt.

Scatter the spring onion and coriander over the top and lightly stir them through, leaving some on the surface. Serve with naan bread and the lemon or lime wedges for squeezing over the lentils.

chicken, coconut and galangal soup

serves 4–6 as a starter

chicken stock

6 **red Asian shallots**

6 slices **galangal**

6 **coriander (cilantro) roots and stems**

500 g (1 lb 2 oz) **chicken wings**

10 **white peppercorns**

10 **makrut (kaffir lime) leaves**, crushed

2 stems **lemon grass**, bruised

8 slices **galangal**

1 large **red chilli**, finely sliced on the diagonal

500 ml (17 fl oz/2 cups) **coconut milk**

2 large **chicken breast fillets**, cut into strips

2 tablespoons **fish sauce**

1 tablespoon **lime juice**

coriander (cilantro) leaves, to serve

To make the chicken stock, put all the ingredients and 2.5 litres (87 fl oz/10 cups) of water in a large saucepan and bring to the boil. Reduce the heat and simmer for 1 hour. Strain.

Put the stock, lime leaves, lemon grass, galangal, chilli and coconut milk in a wok and bring to the boil. Reduce the heat and simmer for 5 minutes. Add the chicken strips and simmer for 5–6 minutes, or until the chicken is cooked. Stir in the fish sauce and lime juice and serve garnished with the coriander leaves.

crab in lime and lemon grass broth with asparagus

serves 4 as a starter

1 tablespoon **vegetable oil**

1–2 teaspoons **chilli paste in soy bean oil**

4 **red Asian shallots**, finely chopped

1 **garlic clove**, finely chopped

200 g (7 oz) fresh **crab meat**

1½ tablespoons **fish sauce**

1 litre (35 fl oz/4 cups) **chicken stock**

2 tablespoons **lime juice**

3 stems **lemon grass**, white part only, 1 bruised, 2 finely chopped

4 **makrut (kaffir lime) leaves**, shredded

250 g (9 oz) **asparagus**, trimmed and cut into 3 cm (1¼ inch) lengths

1 tablespoon shredded **coriander (cilantro) leaves**,
   plus extra sprigs to serve

2 **spring onions (scallions)**, thinly sliced

Heat a wok over medium heat, add the oil and swirl to coat. Stir-fry the chilli paste for about 30 seconds, or until fragrant. Add the shallots and garlic and stir-fry for 30 seconds, or until fragrant and just starting to brown. Stir in the crab meat and 3 teaspoons of fish sauce and stir-fry for 1 minute. Remove from the wok.

Put the chicken stock, lime juice, lemon grass, remaining fish sauce and three of the shredded lime leaves in a clean wok and heat until simmering. Simmer for 10 minutes, then strain to remove the lemon grass and lime leaves.

Return the strained broth to the wok and bring to the boil. Add the asparagus and cook for 2–3 minutes, or until tender but still firm. Add the crab mixture, stirring to combine well, and simmer for 1 minute, or until the crab is heated through. Remove from the heat and stir in the shredded coriander. Season with ground black pepper. Serve topped with coriander sprigs, spring onion and the remaining shredded lime leaf.

pumpkin, prawn and coconut milk soup

serves 4 as a starter

curry paste

1 tablespoon **oil**

1 teaspoon **tamarind concentrate**

2 **garlic cloves**, chopped

4 **red Asian shallots**, chopped

5 **white peppercorns**

2 small **red chillies**

4 **coriander (cilantro) roots**

1 tablespoon chopped **coriander (cilantro) stems**

1 tablespoon chopped **lemon grass**

1 kg (2 lb 4 oz) **raw prawns (shrimp)**

1 tablespoon **oil**

1 **onion**, chopped

2 **garlic cloves**, chopped

1 **carrot**, chopped

2 tablespoons **tomato paste (purée)**

400 ml (14 oz) tin **coconut cream**

800 g (1 lb 12 oz) **pumpkin**, peeled and cut into
1.5 cm (5/8 inch) pieces

270 ml (91/2 fl oz) tin **coconut milk**

11/2 tablespoons **fish sauce**

1 tablespoon grated **palm sugar**

1 handful **Thai basil**

Make a slit down the **back of the prawn** to remove the vein.

Keep the pieces of **pumpkin** small so they **cook quickly**.

To make the curry paste, put all the ingredients in a small food processor or spice grinder and blend until smooth.

Peel the prawns, reserving the shells. Cut a slit down the back of the prawns and remove the vein.

Heat a wok over high heat, add the oil and swirl to coat. Cook the onion, garlic and carrot for 4–5 minutes, or until lightly coloured. Add the prawn shells and cook for 2–3 minutes, or until they turn orange. Add the tomato paste and 1 litre (35 fl oz/ 4 cups) of water, bring to the boil, then reduce the heat and simmer gently for 20 minutes. Don't boil the liquid, otherwise the prawn shells will make it bitter. Strain, reserving the liquid.

Heat a clean wok over high heat, add the paste and cook for 1–2 minutes, or until aromatic. Stir in the coconut cream and cook for 2 minutes. Add the reserved stock, pumpkin and coconut milk and cook for 5 minutes, or until the pumpkin is tender. Add the prawns and cook for 2 minutes, or until cooked. Stir in the fish sauce, palm sugar and basil and serve.

beef rendang

serves 4

curry paste

2 **onions**, roughly chopped

4 **garlic cloves**, peeled

1 tablespoon sliced fresh **ginger**

2 stems **lemon grass**, white part only, sliced

3 small **red chillies**, chopped

2 teaspoons **paprika**

2 teaspoons **ground turmeric**

2 teaspoons **garam masala**

2 teaspoons **ground coriander**

1 kg (2 lb 4 oz) **beef fillet** or **rump steak**, cut into 3 cm (1¼ inch) cubes

2 tablespoons **oil**

3 tablespoons **tamarind purée**

270 ml (9½ fl oz) tin **coconut milk**

2 tablespoons **soft brown sugar**

2 teaspoons **fish sauce**

To make the curry paste, put the onion, garlic, ginger, lemon grass, chilli, paprika, turmeric, garam masala and ground coriander in a blender or food processor and blend until the mixture is smooth.

Put the beef cubes in a bowl. Spoon half the paste onto the beef and mix well to combine. Cover and marinate for at least 2 hours in the refrigerator to allow the flavours to develop.

Heat the oil in a wok, add the beef in batches and stir-fry over medium heat until browned and fragrant. Add the remaining curry paste and cook for 2–3 minutes, or until aromatic.

Stir in the tamarind purée, coconut milk, sugar, fish sauce and 3 tablespoons of water. Bring the mixture to the boil, then reduce the heat and simmer, covered, for 1 hour 15 minutes, or until the meat is tender. Because this is a drier-style curry make sure you stir occasionally during cooking to prevent the curry sticking to the bottom of the wok. Season well and serve with steamed rice.

indian lamb and sweet potato curry

serves 4

1 tablespoon **ghee** or **oil**

1 large **onion**, chopped

3 **garlic cloves**, finely chopped

1 tablespoon grated fresh **ginger**

2–3 tablespoons **rogan josh curry paste**

400 g (14 oz) tin **chopped tomatoes**

8 **curry leaves**

800 g (1 lb 12 oz) **lamb from leg**, cut into 3 cm (1¼ inch) cubes (see tip)

125 g (4½ oz/½ cup) **plain yoghurt**

250 g (9 oz) **orange sweet potato**, peeled and cut into 3 cm (1¼ inch) pieces

40 g (1½ oz/⅓ cup) **slivered almonds**, lightly toasted

1 handful **basil**

Heat the ghee in a wok. Add the onion, garlic and ginger and stir-fry for 3 minutes, or until softened. Add the curry paste and stir-fry for 1 minute, or until aromatic. Stir in the tomatoes, curry leaves, lamb, yoghurt and 125 ml (4 fl oz/½ cup) of water. Bring to the boil, then reduce the heat and simmer, covered, for 1 hour, stirring occasionally to prevent the curry sticking.

Stir in the sweet potato cubes and cook for a further 30 minutes, or until the meat is tender and the sweet potato is cooked. Add a little more water if the sauce is thickening too much.

Garnish with the almonds and basil and serve with jasmine rice.

tip A 1.25 kg (2 lb 12 oz) leg of lamb, boned and trimmed, will give you about 800 g (1 lb 12 oz) of meat.

thai green fish curry

serves 4

curry paste

2 teaspoons **shrimp paste**

2 **long green chillies**, seeded

8 **bird's eye chillies**, seeded

4 **garlic cloves**

4 **red Asian shallots**, peeled

4 **coriander (cilantro) roots**

3 cm (1 1/4 inch) piece **galangal**, chopped

1 stem **lemon grass**, chopped

2 **makrut (kaffir lime) leaves**, finely chopped

1 teaspoon **ground cumin**

1 teaspoon **ground coriander**

5 **white peppercorns**

1 tablespoon **peanut oil**

250 ml (9 fl oz/1 cup) **thick coconut cream**

400 ml (14 fl oz) tin **coconut milk**

6 **makrut (kaffir lime) leaves**, crushed

100 g (3 1/2 oz) **snake beans**, cut into 3 cm (1 1/4 inch) lengths

230 g (8 1/2 oz) tin **bamboo shoots**, drained

200 g (7 oz) **broccoli**, cut into small florets

500 g (1 lb 2 oz) **firm white fish fillets**, cut into 3 cm (1 1/4 inch) pieces

1 handful **Thai basil leaves**

To make the paste, wrap the shrimp paste in foil and toast in a hot wok for 1 minute on each side. Remove the foil and put the shrimp paste in a food processor with the chillies, garlic, shallots, coriander roots, galangal, lemon grass, lime leaves, cumin, coriander, peppercorns, oil and 1 tablespoon of water. Blend until smooth.

Put the coconut cream in a wok and cook over high heat for 5 minutes, or until the oil starts to separate from the cream. Add 3 tablespoons of the curry paste and cook for 2 minutes, or until aromatic. Add the coconut milk, lime leaves, snake beans, bamboo shoots and broccoli and cook for 3–4 minutes. Add the fish and cook for 2–3 minutes, or until cooked through. Stir in the basil and serve with steamed rice. Freeze any leftover paste for next time.

jungle pork curry

serves 4 as part of a spread

curry paste

8–10 large **dried red chillies**

1 tablespoon **shrimp paste**

1 teaspoon **white pepper**

1 stem **lemon grass**, white part only, sliced

5 **red Asian shallots**, sliced

5 **garlic cloves**, crushed

1 tablespoon finely chopped **galangal**

2 teaspoons finely grated fresh **ginger**

2 small **coriander (cilantro) roots**, chopped

1 tablespoon **peanut oil**

1 **garlic clove**, finely chopped

500 g (1 lb 2 oz) **pork fillet**, thinly sliced

500 ml (17 fl oz/2 cups) **chicken stock**

1 tablespoon **fish sauce**

85 g (3 oz) **Thai apple eggplants (aubergines)**, quartered, or **Thai pea eggplants (aubergines)**

100 g (3 1/2 oz) **snake beans**, cut into 3 cm (1 1/4 inch) lengths

60 g (2 1/4 oz/1/4 cup) sliced **bamboo shoots**

4 **kaffir lime (makrut) leaves**, torn

1 small handful **Thai basil leaves**, plus extra to serve

1 **long red chilli**, seeded and julienned

To make the curry paste, soak the dried chillies in boiling water for 10 minutes. Drain and chop. Wrap the shrimp paste in foil and toast in a hot wok for 1 minute on each side. Remove from the foil and put the shrimp paste in a food processor with the chopped chilli and remaining paste ingredients. Add 1 teaspoon of salt and blend until smooth. Add a little water if necessary to form a smooth paste.

Heat a wok over medium heat, add the peanut oil and swirl to coat. Add the garlic and 4 tablespoons of the curry paste and cook, stirring, for 1–2 minutes, or until fragrant. Add the pork and stir-fry for 2–3 minutes, or until browned. Pour in the stock and fish sauce, stir to combine, then bring to the boil. Add the eggplant, snake beans, bamboo shoots and lime leaves, reduce the heat and simmer for 5–8 minutes, or until the vegetables are tender but not soft. Remove from the heat and stir in the basil leaves. Garnish with the chilli strips and extra basil leaves, season to taste with salt, and serve.

aromatic chicken curry

serves 4

2 tablespoons **Madras curry paste**

1 tablespoon **soy sauce**

1 small **red chilli**, seeded and chopped

10 cm (4 inch) piece **lemon grass**

5 cm (2 inch) piece fresh **ginger**, grated

2 **garlic cloves**, chopped

2 tablespoons **tomato paste (purée)**

750 g (1 lb 10 oz) **chicken thigh fillet**, cubed

3 tablespoons **vegetable oil**

2 **red onions**, chopped

400 ml (14 fl oz) tin **coconut milk**

250 g (9 oz/1 punnet) **cherry tomatoes**, halved

1 handful **Thai** or **Italian basil leaves**

Put the curry paste, soy sauce, chilli, lemon grass, ginger, garlic, tomato paste and 1 tablespoon of water in a small food processor and blend to a smooth paste. If you don't have a processor do this either with a mortar and pestle or simply chop everything very finely and combine.

Put the chicken in a bowl, add the paste and mix it all together, rubbing the paste well into the chicken. Cover and marinate in the refrigerator for at least 30 minutes and up to 12 hours.

Heat 2 tablespoons of oil in a wok over medium heat. Add the onion and cook for 10 minutes, or until very soft, but not brown. Remove the onion from the wok. Heat the remaining oil in the wok over high heat. Add the chicken and paste in two batches and stir-fry for 5 minutes, taking care not to burn the paste.

Return the onion and chicken to the wok and add the coconut milk. Bring to the boil, then reduce the heat and simmer, covered, for 20 minutes. Stir in the cherry tomatoes and cook, uncovered, for 5 minutes. Scatter the basil leaves over the top and serve with boiled or steamed rice.

tip Like most curries, this tastes even better if it is left to cool, then refrigerated and reheated either later in the day or the next day.

Basil leaves have an intense flavour. You can use **Thai or Italian** leaves for this dish.

Make sure the chicken is **well coated** in the paste.

chiang mai vegetable curry

serves 4

2 **dried red chillies**

2 teaspoons **coriander seeds**

5 cm (2 inch) piece **galangal**, finely chopped

10 cm (4 inch) piece **lemon grass**, chopped

4 **red Asian shallots**, finely chopped

1 teaspoon **ground cumin**

1/2 teaspoon **ground cinnamon**

3 **garlic cloves**, crushed

5 cm (2 inch) piece fresh **ginger**, finely grated

2 tablespoons **vegetable oil**

1/2 teaspoon **ground turmeric**

3 tablespoons **coconut milk**

200 g (7 oz) fresh **shiitake mushrooms**, roughly chopped

125 g (41/2 oz) **green beans**, trimmed and cut into 5 cm (2 inch) pieces

125 g (41/2 oz) **baby corn**, halved on the diagonal

1 tablespoon **lemon juice**

1 tablespoon **soy sauce**

2 teaspoons **sugar**

2 tablespoons **fish sauce**

65 g (21/4 oz/3/4 cup) **bean sprouts**, tails trimmed

coriander (cilantro) leaves, to serve

Soak the dried chillies in hot water for 10 minutes, then drain and roughly chop. Put the chopped chilli, coriander seeds, galangal, lemon grass, shallots, cumin and cinnamon in a small food processor and grind to a paste, or pound with a mortar and pestle. If it seems too dry, add 1 tablespoon of water. In a separate bowl combine the garlic and ginger.

Heat the oil in a wok over medium heat and cook the garlic and ginger paste for about 30 seconds. Add the curry paste and cook for 2 minutes, or until aromatic.

Add one by one, stirring well after each addition, the ground turmeric, coconut milk, mushrooms, beans, baby corn, lemon juice, soy sauce, sugar, fish sauce and 250 ml (9 fl oz/1 cup) of boiling water. Cook for 2 minutes then serve, garnished with the bean sprouts and coriander leaves. Delicious with noodles or rice.

tip This aromatic hot and spicy curry is suitable for vegetarians if you replace the fish sauce with 1 tablespoon of light soy sauce.

panang chicken

serves 4

curry paste
6 long **dried red chillies**
4 **red Asian shallots**, roughly chopped
6 **garlic cloves**, roughly chopped
3 stems **lemon grass**, roughly chopped
6 cm (2 1/2 inch) piece **galangal**, roughly
   chopped
1 teaspoon **ground coriander**
2 teaspoons **ground cumin**
6 **coriander (cilantro) roots**, chopped
2 teaspoons **shrimp paste**
4 tablespoons toasted **peanuts**
1 tablespoon **vegetable oil**

2 tablespoons **vegetable oil**
2 **garlic cloves**, crushed
400 ml (14 fl oz) tin **coconut milk**
1 tablespoon **fish sauce**
2 teaspoons **light brown sugar**
   or **palm sugar**
600 g (1 lb 5 oz) **chicken breast fillet**,
   cut into strips
1 handful **coriander (cilantro) leaves**
1 **long green chilli**, seeded and
   cut into thin strips

To make the curry paste, soak the chillies in hot water for 10 minutes, then discard the water and roughly chop the chillies. Put into a small blender with the shallots, garlic, lemon grass, galangal, spices, coriander roots, shrimp paste, peanuts and oil and process to a paste. Alternatively, put all the ingredients in a mortar and pestle, gradually adding each ingredient once the previous one is quite crushed, and grind to a paste. Remove 3 tablespoons of paste and freeze the rest for next time.

Heat the oil in a large wok over low–medium heat. Add the garlic and curry paste and stir-fry for 4–5 minutes, or until aromatic. Be careful not to burn the paste or the garlic. Add the coconut milk, increase the heat to medium and simmer for about 5 minutes. Stir in the fish sauce and sugar, then add the chicken strips and cook, covered, for 10 minutes, or until the chicken is cooked through. Serve on steamed rice, garnished with coriander leaves and strips of green chilli.

tip This paste recipe makes 3–4 times as much as you need. Put the rest in a ziplock plastic bag and freeze ready for next time. Once the paste is made this is a really speedy curry.

vietnamese pork curry

serves 4

3 tablespoons **peanut oil**

1 large **onion**, cut into slices from top to bottom

3 **garlic cloves**, crushed

2 cm (3/4 inch) piece **galangal**, grated

2 small **red chillies**, finely chopped

1 stem **lemon grass**, finely chopped

3 tablespoons **mild curry powder** (see tip)

1 kg (2 lb 4 oz) **pork shoulder**, cut into cubes

400 ml (14 fl oz) tin **coconut milk**

1 tablespoon **lime juice**

450 g (1 lb) **taro** or **white sweet potato**, peeled and cut into 3 cm (1¼ inch) cubes

40 g (1½ oz/¼ cup) toasted **unsalted peanuts**, chopped

1 small handful **Vietnamese mint leaves**, torn

1 small handful **sawleaf (sawtooth) herb leaves**, torn (see tip)

Heat the oil in a large wok over high heat, add the onion slices and stir-fry for 3–4 minutes, or until soft and the edges have browned. Add the garlic, galangal, chilli and lemon grass and cook for 1–2 minutes.

Add the curry powder and pork and cook, stirring, for 3–4 minutes, or until the pork loses its pink colour. Stir in the coconut milk and simmer gently, uncovered, for about 45 minutes. Stir the curry occasionally and make sure the liquid doesn't evaporate too quickly.

Add the lime juice and taro and cook for a further 30 minutes. To serve, scatter the chopped peanuts over the curry and pile the mint leaves and sawleaf on top.

tips Mild curry powder is available from Vietnamese or Asian grocers if you can't get it at the supermarket. Sawleaf is a herb with serrated leaves about 5 cm (2 inches) long. It tastes similar to coriander (cilantro), so if you are unable to find it, you can use coriander instead.

butter prawn curry

serves 4

50 g (1³/4 oz) **ghee** or **butter**

1 **onion**, cut into wedges

2 **garlic cloves**, crushed

2 teaspoons **ground cumin**

1 teaspoon **mild paprika**

2 teaspoons **garam masala**

2 teaspoons **ground coriander**

2 tablespoons **tandoori paste**

2 tablespoons **tomato paste (purée)**

200 g (7 oz/1 cup) **crushed tomatoes**

300 ml (10¹/2 fl oz) **pouring (single) cream**

250 ml (9 fl oz/1 cup) **coconut cream**

1 **cinnamon stick**

750 g (1 lb 10 oz) **raw prawns (shrimp)**,
    peeled and deveined, tails intact

2 teaspoons **sugar**

1 tablespoon **lemon juice**

coriander (cilantro) leaves, to serve

Heat a wok over high heat, add the ghee and swirl to coat. Add the onion and cook for 2–3 minutes to soften, then add the garlic, cumin, paprika, garam masala and ground coriander and cook for 30 seconds.

Stir in the tandoori and tomato pastes and cook for 1 minute, stirring constantly. Add the crushed tomatoes, cream, coconut cream and cinnamon stick and cook for 5 minutes, or until thickened.

Add the prawns and cook for 2–3 minutes, or until pink and cooked through. Stir in the sugar and lemon juice. Garnish with the coriander and serve with basmati rice.

malaysian beef curry

serves 4

1 1/2 tablespoons **tamarind pulp**

25 g (1 oz/1/4 cup) **desiccated coconut**

4–5 small **red chillies**, seeded and
roughly chopped

6 **red Asian shallots**, quartered

4 **garlic cloves**

4 **candlenuts** or **macadamia nuts**

3 tablespoons **vegetable oil**

1 teaspoon **ground turmeric**

1 teaspoon **ground cumin**

1 teaspoon **ground coriander**

1/2 teaspoon **ground cinnamon**

1 kg (2 lb 4 oz) **chuck steak**, cut
into cubes

2 strips **lemon zest**

2 **tomatoes**, chopped

1 teaspoon **soft brown sugar**

400 ml (14 fl oz) tin **coconut milk**

Put the tamarind pulp in a small bowl with 3 tablespoons of very hot water and leave for 10 minutes. Mash the tamarind with a fork to dissolve, then strain through a fine sieve, reserving the liquid and discarding the pulp.

Dry-fry the desiccated coconut in a large wok for 1–2 minutes, or until golden brown. Set aside for later.

Purée the chilli, shallots, garlic and candlenuts in a food processor. Heat the oil in the wok over medium heat and cook the chilli purée, stirring, for 1 minute. Stir in the turmeric, cumin, coriander and cinnamon and cook for 3 minutes. Add the steak cubes and cook, stirring occasionally, for 5 minutes.

Stir in the lemon zest, tomato, sugar, coconut milk, tamarind liquid and toasted coconut. Simmer, uncovered, for 1 1/2–2 hours, or until the beef is very tender and the gravy has reduced. Stir occasionally during cooking. Serve with boiled or steamed rice.

burmese lamb with yoghurt

serves 4

3 cm (1¼ inch) piece fresh **ginger**, roughly chopped

3–4 **green bird's eye chillies**, seeded and roughly chopped

5 **garlic cloves**

3 large handfuls **coriander (cilantro) leaves**, roughly chopped

1 teaspoon **salt**

1 teaspoon **ground turmeric**

1 teaspoon **ground cumin**

1½ tablespoons **lemon juice**

1 kg (2 lb 4 oz) boned **leg of lamb**, cut into cubes

2 teaspoons **whole aniseeds** or **fennel seeds**

3 tablespoons **vegetable oil**

1 large **onion**, chopped

3 **curry leaves**

500 g (1 lb 2 oz/2 cups) **plain yoghurt**

Aniseeds have a **similar flavour** to fennel seeds, so use these if you can't get them.

Cook the onions over **very low heat** so they do not burn.

Put the ginger, chilli, garlic, coriander, salt, turmeric and cumin in a blender or small processor and process until fine. Add the lemon juice and blend to a smooth purée. Transfer to a large bowl and add the lamb. Toss to coat well, then cover and set aside at room temperature for 1–1 1/2 hours.

Heat a large wok over medium heat and dry-fry the aniseeds, stirring, for 1 minute, or until fragrant. Transfer to a bowl and set aside. Add the oil to the wok and when it is hot, stir in the onion. Reduce the heat to low and cook for 7–8 minutes, or until soft and lightly golden. Toss in the curry leaves.

Add the lamb and its marinade and cook over high heat for 3–4 minutes, stirring often, until the spices brown on the base of the wok. Add the aniseeds and stir in 500 ml (17 fl oz/2 cups) of water. Bring to the boil, then reduce the heat to low and simmer, covered, for 30 minutes. Remove the lid and simmer gently for another 30 minutes. The curry will be quite dry.

Add the yoghurt and roughly stir it through, leaving some blobs. Cook until it is heated through but do not boil. Remove from the heat and rest for about 5 minutes before serving. The yoghurt may separate if the curry is reheated, but this does not affect the flavour.

pumpkin bhaji

serves 4 as part of a spread, or 2 as a main course

2 tablespoons **vegetable oil**

1 teaspoon **yellow mustard seeds**

1 **onion,** finely chopped

1 teaspoon grated fresh **ginger**

1 **green chilli,** seeded and chopped

1 teaspoon **ground coriander**

1/2 teaspoon **garam masala**

1/2 teaspoon **ground turmeric**

1/2 teaspoon **ground cumin**

1/2 teaspoon **chilli flakes**

750 g (1 lb 10 oz) **pumpkin,** peeled, seeded
    and cut into 3 cm (11/4 inch) cubes

400 g (14 oz) tin **chopped tomatoes**

2 teaspoons **soft brown sugar**

3 tablespoons **plain yoghurt**

coriander (cilantro) leaves, to serve

Heat the oil in a large wok and cook the mustard seeds until they just start to pop. Add the onion, ginger and chilli and stir-fry for 2 minutes. Add the coriander, garam masala, turmeric, cumin and chilli flakes and stir-fry for 1 minute, or until aromatic.

Stir in the pumpkin, chopped tomatoes, sugar and 125 ml (4 fl oz/1/2 cup) of water. Bring to the boil, then reduce the heat and simmer, covered, for 30 minutes, or until the pumpkin is tender. Stir occasionally. Gently fold in the yoghurt and scatter with coriander leaves before serving with boiled rice.

red chicken curry

serves 4

540 ml (18½ fl oz) **coconut milk**

2 tablespoons **red curry paste**

5 cm (2 inch) piece fresh **ginger**, peeled and julienned

125 ml (4 fl oz/½ cup) **chicken stock** or **water**

4 **makrut (kaffir lime) leaves**

600 g (1 lb 5 oz) **chicken breast fillets**, cut into thin strips

125 g (4½ oz) **green beans**, trimmed and cut into
   5 cm (2 inch) pieces on the diagonal

2 tablespoons **fish sauce**

1 tablespoon shaved **palm sugar**

1 tablespoon **lime juice**

1 large **red chilli**, thinly sliced on the diagonal

coriander (cilantro) leaves, to serve

Heat a wok over medium heat. Add 2 tablespoons of the thick liquid from the top of the coconut milk and the red curry paste and ginger. Cook over low heat for 2 minutes, or until fragrant. Stir in the remaining coconut milk, the stock and lime leaves. Bring to the boil, then reduce the heat and simmer for 10 minutes, or until the mixture is reduced and thickened a little.

Add the chicken and green beans. Simmer for 5 minutes, or until the chicken is cooked and the beans are just tender. Stir in the fish sauce, palm sugar and lime juice. Garnish with the chilli and coriander leaves and serve with jasmine rice.

vietnamese-style seafood curry

serves 4

curry paste

1 tablespoon **coriander seeds**

2 teaspoons **cumin seeds**

1 teaspoon **dried chilli flakes**

2 teaspoons **shrimp paste**

4 **garlic cloves**, chopped

2 stems **lemon grass**, white part only, chopped

2 cm (3/4 inch) piece fresh **turmeric**, chopped

5 **spring onions (scallions)**, chopped

3 cm (1 1/4 inch) piece fresh **ginger**, chopped

2 tablespoons **vegetable oil**

400 ml (14 fl oz) tin **coconut cream**

125 ml (4 fl oz/1/2 cup) **chicken stock**

3 cm (1 1/4 inch) piece **galangal**, sliced

600 g (1 lb 5 oz) **pumpkin**, peeled, seeded and cut into 2 cm (3/4 inch) pieces

300 g (10 1/2 oz) **firm white fish fillets**, cut into 2.5 cm (1 inch) pieces

16 **raw prawns (shrimp)**, peeled and deveined, tails intact

12 **scallops** without roe

1 1/2 tablespoons **fish sauce**

1 small handful **Vietnamese mint**, torn

To make the curry paste, put the coriander and cumin seeds and chilli in a hot wok and dry-fry over high heat for 30 seconds, or until aromatic. Transfer to a spice grinder and grind to a powder. Wrap the shrimp paste in foil and heat in a hot wok for 1 minute on each side. Add to the spices in the grinder with the garlic, lemon grass, turmeric, spring onion, ginger, oil and 1 tablespoon of water and grind to a smooth paste.

Heat a wok over high heat, add the paste and cook for 1 minute, or until aromatic. Add the coconut cream, stock, galangal and pumpkin and cook over high heat for 4–5 minutes, or until the pumpkin is tender.

Add the fish, prawns and scallops and cook for 2–3 minutes, or until cooked through. Stir in the fish sauce and mint and serve with rice.

indian-style beef curry

serves 4

60 g (2¹/4 oz) **ghee**

2 **onions**, chopped

2 **garlic cloves**, crushed

3 small **red chillies**, finely chopped

1 teaspoon **ground turmeric**

2 teaspoons **garam masala**

2 teaspoons **ground coriander**

1 teaspoon **ground cumin**

10 **cardamom pods**, lightly crushed

1/4 teaspoon **ground cloves**

1 kg (2 lb 4 oz) **chuck steak**, cut into cubes

140 ml (5 fl oz) tin **coconut milk**

2 **bay leaves**

2 **large potatoes**, cut into 3 cm (1¹/4 inch) chunks

Melt the ghee in a large wok over low heat, add the onion and cook, stirring occasionally, for 5–6 minutes, or until soft and golden. Add the garlic and chilli and cook until aromatic.

Stir in the turmeric, garam masala, coriander, cumin, cardamom pods, cloves and 1 tablespoon of hot water and cook for 5 minutes. Stir in the beef and cook over high heat, stirring often, for 5 minutes.

Add the coconut milk, bay leaves, 1 teaspoon of salt and 375 ml (13 fl oz/1¹/2 cups) of water. Simmer, covered, for 45 minutes. Scoop out and discard the cardamom pods floating on the surface. Add the potatoes and 125 ml (4 fl oz/1/2 cup) of water and cook, uncovered, for a further 45 minutes. Like many curries, this is even better the following day. Serve with boiled basmati rice.

thai yellow vegetable curry

serves 4

yellow curry paste

8 small **green chillies**

5 **red Asian shallots**, roughly chopped,

1 stem **lemon grass**, white part only,
   finely chopped

2 **garlic cloves**, crushed

2 tablespoons finely chopped **galangal**

1 tablespoon **lime juice**

1 tablespoon finely chopped **coriander
(cilantro) stem and root**

1 teaspoon **ground coriander**

1 teaspoon **ground cumin**

1/2 teaspoon **ground turmeric**

1/2 teaspoon **black peppercorns**

2 tablespoons **peanut oil**

500 ml (17 fl oz/2 cups) **coconut cream**

125 ml (4 fl oz/1/2 cup) **vegetable stock**

150 g (51/2 oz) **snake beans**, cut into
   3 cm (11/4 inch) lengths

150 g (51/2 oz) fresh **baby corn**

1 **slender eggplant (aubergine)**, cut
   into 1 cm (1/2 inch) slices

100 g (31/2 oz) **cauliflower**, cut into
   small florets

2 small **zucchini (courgettes)**, cut into
   1 cm (1/2 inch) slices

1 small **red capsicum (pepper)**, cut
   into 1 cm (1/2 inch) slices

11/2 tablespoons **fish sauce**

1 teaspoon grated **palm sugar**

chopped **red chilli**, to garnish

coriander (cilantro) leaves, to garnish

To make the curry paste, put all the ingredients in a food processor or mortar and pestle. Process or grind to a smooth paste.

Heat a wok over medium heat, add the oil and swirl to coat. Add 2 tablespoons of the curry paste and cook for 1 minute. Add half the coconut cream. Bring to the boil, then reduce the heat and simmer for 10 minutes, or until thick and the oil starts to separate from the cream.

Add the stock, vegetables and remaining coconut cream and cook for 5 minutes, or until the vegetables are tender. Stir in the fish sauce and palm sugar. Garnish with chilli and coriander and serve with steamed rice.

mussaman lamb curry

serves 4

curry paste

1 tablespoon **coriander seeds**

2 teaspoons **cumin seeds**

1 teaspoon **cardamom seeds** or

   1 teaspoon **ground cardamom**

1 **cinnamon stick**, broken

10 small **dried red chillies**, seeds

   removed

2 teaspoons **shrimp paste**

8 **red Asian shallots**, peeled

4 **garlic cloves**

1 stem **lemon grass**, chopped

3 slices **galangal**, chopped

1 tablespoon **vegetable oil**

250 ml (9 fl oz/1 cup) **thick coconut**

   cream

750 g (1 lb 10 oz) **lamb fillets**,

   cut into 2 cm (3/4 inch) pieces

400 ml (14 fl oz) tin **coconut milk**

4 **cardamom pods**, bruised

1 tablespoon grated **palm sugar**

1 1/2 tablespoons **fish sauce**

15 g (1/2 oz/1/4 cup) toasted **candlenuts**

   or **macadamia nuts**, chopped

sliced **red and green chillies**,

   to serve

To make the curry paste, heat a wok over high heat, add the coriander, cumin and cardamom seeds, cinnamon stick and dried chillies and dry-fry for 1 minute, or until aromatic. Transfer to a spice grinder and grind to a powder.

Wrap the shrimp paste in foil and heat in a hot wok for 1 minute on each side. Put in a small food processor with the ground spices and remaining paste ingredients and process to a smooth paste.

Put the coconut cream in a wok and cook over high heat for 5 minutes, or until the oil starts to separate from the cream. Add half the paste and cook for 2–3 minutes. Add the lamb and cook for 2 minutes, then stir in the coconut milk and cardamom pods and cook for 4–5 minutes, or until the lamb is tender. Stir in the sugar, fish sauce and candlenuts. Garnish with the sliced chilli and serve with steamed rice.

tip The recipe for the curry paste makes 125 g (4 1/2 oz/1/2 cup), which is enough for two curries, so freeze the leftover paste and use it another time.

braised tofu with pork

serves 4 as part of a spread, or 2 as a main course

1/2 teaspoon **Sichuan peppercorns**

1 tablespoon **oil**

4 **spring onions (scallions)**, thinly sliced on the diagonal

3 cm (1 1/4 inch) piece fresh **ginger**, julienned

2 large **garlic cloves**, crushed

500 g (1 lb 2 oz) **pork fillet**, trimmed and cut into
    2 cm (3/4 inch) pieces

4 tablespoons **honey soy sauce**

4 tablespoons **rice wine vinegar**

2 tablespoons **soft brown sugar**

3 **star anise**

300 g (10 1/2 oz) **silken firm tofu**, cut into 3 cm (1 1/4 inch) pieces

1 large handful **coriander (cilantro) leaves**

Heat a wok over high heat and dry-fry the peppercorns for 1 minute. Remove and grind to a powder in a spice grinder or mortar and pestle. Add the oil to the wok and swirl to coat. Cook the spring onion, ginger, garlic and pepper for 1 minute, then add the pork and cook for 2 minutes, or until browned.

Combine the soy sauce, vinegar and sugar with 125 ml (4 fl oz/1/2 cup) of water and add to the wok with the star anise and tofu. Reduce the heat and simmer, covered, for 10 minutes, or until the pork is tender. Stir in the coriander and serve with rice.

red miso chicken wok-pot

serves 4

2 tablespoons **vegetable oil**

750 g (1 lb 10 oz) **skinless chicken thigh fillets,**
   trimmed and halved

2 tablespoons julienned fresh **ginger**

4 **star anise**

1 **cinnamon stick**

1 tablespoon **sake**

2 tablespoons **mirin**

2 teaspoons **Japanese rice vinegar**

125 ml (4 fl oz/1/2 cup) **chicken stock**

2 tablespoons **Japanese soy sauce**

1 tablespoon **red miso paste**

3 **spring onions (scallions),** green part only,
   finely sliced on the diagonal into 3 cm (11/4 inch) slices

Heat a wok until very hot, add half the oil and swirl to coat. Add the chicken fillets in batches and cook over high heat for 2 minutes on each side, or until browned. Remove from the wok.

Reduce the heat to medium, add extra oil if necessary and stir-fry the ginger, star anise and cinnamon stick for 30 seconds. Add the sake, mirin and vinegar and quickly stir until they evaporate. Pour in the stock, soy sauce and 125 ml (4 fl oz/ 1/2 cup) of water, bring to a simmer and cook, stirring, for 2 minutes. Stir in the miso paste, return the chicken to the wok and simmer for about 15–20 minutes, or until the chicken is cooked through and tender. Garnish with the spring onion and serve.

spicy prawns in coconut cream

serves 4

1 tablespoon **vegetable oil**

1 tablespoon **Madras** or **hot curry paste**

1 small **onion**, finely chopped

2 **garlic cloves**, crushed

1 **red chilli**, seeded and finely chopped

2 ripe **tomatoes**, chopped

1 tablespoon **lime juice**

200 ml (7 fl oz) **coconut cream**

24 **raw prawns (shrimp)**, peeled and deveined,
   tails removed

Heat the oil in a wok over low heat. Add the curry paste and stir-fry for 1 minute, or until aromatic, but make sure it doesn't burn. Increase the heat, add the onion, garlic and chilli and cook, stirring frequently, for about 5 minutes.

Add the tomato and lime juice and cook for 2 minutes, or until the tomato has softened and broken down. Stir in the coconut cream and bring slowly to the boil. Add the prawns and cook for 3 minutes, or until they turn pink. Serve immediately with rice or bread.

satay lamb

serves 4

3 tablespoons **peanut oil**

750 g (1 lb 10 oz) **lamb backstraps** or **loin fillet**, thinly sliced

2 teaspoons **ground cumin**

1 teaspoon **ground turmeric**

1 **red capsicum (pepper)**, sliced

3 tablespoons **mild sweet chilli sauce**

3 tablespoons **crunchy peanut butter**

250 ml (9 fl oz/1 cup) **coconut milk**

2 teaspoons **soft brown sugar**

1–2 tablespoons **lemon juice**

1 small handful **coriander (cilantro) leaves**, roughly chopped

40 g (1 1/2 oz/1/4 cup) toasted **unsalted peanuts**, chopped

Heat 1 tablespoon of oil in a wok and stir-fry the lamb in batches for 3 minutes, or until browned. Remove from the wok.

Heat the remaining oil in the wok, add the cumin, turmeric and capsicum and stir-fry for 2 minutes, or until the capsicum is slightly tender.

Return the lamb to the wok and stir in the sweet chilli sauce, peanut butter, coconut milk and sugar. Bring the mixture to boil, then reduce the heat and simmer for 5 minutes, or until the meat is tender and the sauce has thickened slightly. Remove from the heat and stir in the lemon juice, to taste. Garnish with coriander and peanuts, and serve with steamed rice.

vegetable laksa

serves 4

250 g (9 oz) **dried rice vermicelli**

1 tablespoon **vegetable oil**

3 tablespoons **laksa paste**

750 ml (26 fl oz/3 cups) **coconut milk**

750 ml (26 fl oz/3 cups) good-quality **vegetable** or **chicken stock**

90 g (3¼ oz/½ cup) **baby corn**, halved diagonally

2 **snake beans**, cut into 4 cm (1½ inch) lengths

¼ **Chinese cabbage (wong bok)**, shredded

4 **fried tofu puffs**, halved

150 g (5½ oz/1⅔ cups) **bean sprouts**, tails trimmed

1 **Lebanese (short) cucumber**, julienned

3 tablespoons coarsely chopped **Vietnamese mint**

1 small **red chilli**, thinly sliced

Put the vermicelli in a bowl and cover with boiling water. Heat the oil in a large wok over medium heat and cook the laksa paste for 1–2 minutes, or until fragrant. Stir in the coconut milk and stock and bring to the boil. Add the baby corn and snake beans and simmer for 2–3 minutes. Stir in the cabbage.

Drain the vermicelli, rinse under hot water and drain again. Spoon into four deep serving bowls. Divide the tofu puffs, bean sprouts and cucumber among the bowls. Ladle the vegetables and broth into the bowls and scatter the mint leaves and chilli over the top.

mee siam

serves 4

120 g (4¹/2 oz) **dried rice vermicelli**

1 tablespoon **shrimp paste**

4 **red Asian shallots**, peeled

3 **garlic cloves**, crushed

8 long **dried red chillies**, soaked in boiling water
for 10 minutes, seeds removed

2 teaspoons **dried shrimp**, soaked in boiling water
for 10 minutes, drained

3 tablespoons **peanut oil**

12 **raw king prawns (shrimp)**, peeled and deveined,
tails intact

90 g (3¹/4 oz/1 cup) **bean sprouts**, tails trimmed

broth

85 g (3 oz/¹/3 cup) **yellow bean sauce (taucheo)**

2¹/2 tablespoons **tamarind purée**

1 teaspoon **caster (superfine) sugar**

1 **onion**, halved, finely sliced horizontally into half rings

to serve

8 **fried square tofu puffs**, halved diagonally

2 hard-boiled **eggs**, quartered

2 **limes**, cut into wedges

4 **garlic chives**, snipped

crisp fried shallots, to serve

Put the noodles in a bowl, cover with boiling water and soak for 5 minutes. Drain well and set aside. Wrap the shrimp paste in foil and toast in a hot wok for 1 minute on each side. Remove the foil and put the paste in a food processor with the shallots, garlic, dried chillies and dried shrimp. Blend to form a paste, adding water if necessary.

Heat a wok over high heat, add 1 tablespoon of oil and swirl to coat. Stir-fry the prawns for 2–3 minutes, or until pink and cooked through. Remove. Add another tablespoon of oil and stir-fry the paste for 1 minute, or until fragrant. Remove half the paste and set aside. Add 250 ml (9 fl oz/1 cup) of water to the wok with salt, to taste. Stir to combine and bring to a simmer. Add the noodles and cook for about 3–4 minutes, then add the bean sprouts and cook for 1 minute, or until all the liquid evaporates.

Meanwhile, to make the broth, combine the ingredients in a saucepan with 1 litre (35 fl oz/4 cups) of water and bring to the boil. Add the reserved spice paste, stirring well, then simmer for 5 minutes.

To serve, divide the noodle mixture among four deep serving bowls. Ladle on the broth, then top each bowl with prawns, tofu puffs, boiled eggs and lime wedges. Garnish with the chives and crisp fried shallots and serve immediately.

Don't **overcook** the **prawns** or they will become tough and rubbery.

Add the **bean sprouts** and cook just until the water **evaporates**.

braised beef with sesame water spinach

serves 4

2 tablespoons **fish sauce**

2 tablespoons **kecap manis**

1 stem **lemon grass**, white part only, finely chopped

4 **coriander (cilantro) roots**, finely chopped

2 **garlic cloves**, finely chopped

4 tablespoons **vegetable oil**

500 g (1 lb 2 oz) **beef fillet**, in one piece

3 teaspoons **white sesame seeds**

250 g (9 oz) **water spinach (ong choy)**,
    cut into 5 cm (2 inch) lengths

1 teaspoon **sesame oil**

1 handful **coriander (cilantro) leaves**

Combine the fish sauce, kecap manis, lemon grass, coriander roots, garlic and 2 tablespoons of the oil in a bowl. Add the piece of beef and turn to coat. Cover the bowl with plastic wrap and refrigerate overnight.

Drain the beef, reserving the marinade. Dry with paper towels and cut into 1 cm (1/2 inch) thick slices. Heat a wok and dry-fry the sesame seeds over medium heat for about 2 minutes, or until golden. Remove from the wok.

Heat 1 tablespoon of oil in the wok and add the water spinach. Cook over high heat for about 2 minutes, or until the stems are tender. Add the sesame oil and sesame seeds and toss well. Transfer to a serving plate and keep warm.

Heat the remaining oil over high heat, add the beef in batches and stir-fry for 2–3 minutes. Return all the beef to the wok. Add the reserved marinade and 125 ml (4 fl oz/1/2 cup) of water, reduce the heat to medium and cook, stirring often, for 5–6 minutes. Spoon the beef over the water spinach, pile the coriander on top and serve with jasmine rice.

good fortune clams

serves 4

100 g (3¹/2 oz) **dried rice vermicelli**

3 tablespoons **vegetable oil**

3 **garlic cloves**, crushed

2–3 teaspoons **black bean chilli sauce (spicy black bean sauce)**

1 kg (2 lb 4 oz) **clams (vongole)**, soaked and cleaned

3 tablespoons **Chinese rice wine**

3 tablespoons **chicken stock**

2 teaspoons **light soy sauce**

3 tablespoons chopped **coriander (cilantro) leaves**

Soak the vermicelli in boiling water for 5 minutes. Drain well.

Heat a wok over medium–high heat, add the oil and swirl to coat. Stir-fry the garlic and black bean chilli sauce for about 30 seconds, or until fragrant. Add the clams, rice wine, stock and soy sauce. Increase the heat to high, then cover the wok with a lid and cook the clams, gently shaking occasionally, for 3–5 minutes, or until the clams have opened up.

Remove from the heat and discard any unopened clams. Add the vermicelli and toss gently. Scatter the chopped coriander over the top, toss gently and serve.

braised pork belly in ground bean sauce

serves 4

750 g (1 lb 10 oz) **pork belly,** cut into 2 x 8 cm
 (3/4 x 31/4 inch) portions (choose belly with no ribs)

2 tablespoons **oil**

2 **garlic cloves**, chopped

2 cm (3/4 inch) piece fresh **ginger**, chopped

2 tablespoons **ground bean sauce** (see tip)

1 large cube of **red bean curd** (see tip)

11/2 tablespoons **oyster sauce**

2 teaspoons **soy sauce**

3 tablespoons **sugar**

2 **star anise**

Fill a wok three-quarters full of water and bring to the boil. Add the pieces of pork belly and simmer for 3–4 minutes, then drain.

Heat the oil in a wok over medium heat. Add the garlic and ginger and stir-fry for 1 minute, or until aromatic. Add the ground bean sauce, bean curd, pork, oyster sauce, soy sauce, sugar, star anise and 310 ml (11 fl oz) of water. Bring to the boil, then cover with a tight-fitting lid. If your wok does not have a particularly tight-fitting lid, or doesn't have a lid at all, cover it with foil first and then an appropriate-sized lid from another pan. Simmer for 1–11/4 hours, or until the meat is tender and the sauce has reduced and thickened. If the liquid evaporates too quickly add a little extra water.

Serve hot with steamed rice and a vegetable side dish.

tip Ground bean sauce and red bean curd are both readily available from Asian food stores.

chiang mai noodles

serves 4–6

200 g (7 oz) **thin dried egg noodles**

1 tablespoon **vegetable oil**

1 **red onion**, chopped

2 **garlic cloves**, finely chopped

2–3 tablespoons **red curry paste**

1 teaspoon **ground turmeric**

400 ml (14 fl oz) tin **coconut milk**

425 g (15 oz) **chicken breast fillet**, cut into thin strips

2 tablespoons **fish sauce**

1 tablespoon **palm sugar**

juice of 1 **lime**

50 g (1³/4 oz) packet **fried egg noodles**, roughly broken up

2 **spring onions (scallions)**, thinly shredded

1 small handful **coriander (cilantro) leaves**

crisp fried shallots, to serve

Cook the noodles in a large saucepan of boiling water for 4 minutes. Drain under cold water.

Heat the oil in a large wok. Add the onion and garlic and stir-fry for 2 minutes, or until lightly browned. Stir in the curry paste and turmeric and stir-fry for 1 minute, or until fragrant. Add the coconut milk and 500 ml (17 fl oz/2 cups) of water. Bring to the boil, then reduce the heat and simmer for 5 minutes.

Add the chicken strips and simmer for 5 minutes, or until the chicken is cooked. Stir in the fish sauce, palm sugar and lime juice and simmer for 1–2 minutes, or until the sugar has dissolved.

Divide the cooked egg noodles among four to six deep bowls and ladle on the chicken and coconut mixture. Top with the fried noodles, spring onion, coriander leaves and crisp fried shallots.

pork in yellow bean and coconut sauce

serves 4

560 ml (20 fl oz) **coconut cream**

125 ml (4 fl oz/1/2 cup) **yellow bean sauce (taucheo)**,
  slightly mashed with a fork

21/2 tablespoons **palm sugar**

1 tablespoon **tamarind concentrate**

1 teaspoon **fish sauce**

500 g (1 lb 2 oz) **pork fillet**, chopped into 4 cm (11/2 inch) pieces

3 **red Asian shallots**, sliced

1 small **red chilli**, sliced

1 handful **coriander (cilantro) leaves**

Put 125 ml (4 fl oz/1/2 cup) of coconut cream in a wok and heat until it 'cracks' and separates (this is where the oil separates from the coconut milk). Stir in the yellow bean sauce, palm sugar, tamarind, fish sauce and the remaining coconut cream. Bring to the boil, then reduce to a simmer and add the pork. Cook for 10 minutes.

Add the shallots and chilli and cook a further 5 minutes. Garnish with the coriander leaves and serve with steamed rice.

braised chicken with vegetables

serves 4

3 **chicken thighs**

3 **chicken drumsticks**

2 tablespoons **vegetable oil**

8 **baby leeks**, white part only, cleaned and cut into 1 cm (1/2 inch) slices

6 **red Asian shallots**, quartered

100 g (31/2 oz) fresh **shiitake mushrooms**, thickly sliced

juice of 1 **mandarin** (or 4 tablespoons **orange juice**)

2 tablespoons **soy sauce**

2 tablespoons **dry sherry**

2 teaspoons **soft brown sugar**

2 teaspoons **green peppercorns**

1 teaspoon **sesame oil**

2 **baby bok choy (pak choy)**, quartered lengthways

Chop the chicken thighs and legs into bite-sized pieces through the bone (this is best done with a Chinese cleaver). Heat the oil in a large wok and brown the chicken in batches over high heat for 1–2 minutes. Remove from the wok.

Add the leek and shallots and stir-fry for 1 minute. Add the mushrooms, stir-fry for 1 minute, then add the mandarin juice, soy sauce, sherry, sugar, peppercorns and 125 ml (4 fl oz/1/2 cup) of water.

Return the chicken pieces to the wok. Reduce the heat and simmer, covered, for 20 minutes, or until the chicken is tender. Add the sesame oil and bok choy and cook, stirring, for 1 minute, or until wilted. Serve with steamed rice.

steaming

the benefits of steaming

Steaming is one of the gentlest ways to cook food and it really is a healthy option as the food is cooked by moist heat rather than in oil or fat. When you steam food it retains its inherent texture, shape and taste. In addition, steaming can invigorate dried or tough food by adding moisture and tenderness. Many foods are steamed in a wrapping of banana, lotus or bamboo leaves, both to act as a useful container and to keep the food moist during cooking. There are two methods of steaming. The most common involves cooking food over boiling liquid in an enclosed environment. The second method is to add a little water to a wok or pan, add the food, then cover with a lid and put the wok over the heat, with the steam from the evaporated liquid cooking the food.

why use a wok to steam?

A wok's broad sides and concave shape allow for a large surface area of water to produce steam, and enough room for the steam to circulate freely and cook the food. Make sure the wok is firmly balanced on the stovetop to avoid the hazards of spilled boiling water. It is best to use a flat-bottomed wok with two handles, and to be extra safe, it is worth investing in a wok stand. An electric wok also works well.

Many Chinese cooks use separate woks for steaming and stir-frying because the hot water used for steaming strips off the seasoning layer that is so valued when stir-frying.

bamboo steamers and other options

Asian bamboo steamers are great for steaming; they are cheap, effective and can double as a serving vessel. Other options include stainless steel and aluminium steamers. Metal steamers are easier to clean and maintain than bamboo, but they are also more expensive and lack the aesthetic appeal of bamboo steamers. Another option is to use a heatproof dish. If you are using a bowl or plate, you'll need to rest it on a round cake rack that fits inside the wok about halfway down — the idea is to prevent the plate from touching the water. Be aware that some porcelain or ceramic dishes may crack if used for steaming. To prevent this happening, put a cake rack in the wok, then sit the dish on top. Add enough water to completely cover the dish, cover with a lid and bring the water to the boil. Boil for 10 minutes, then turn off the heat and allow the wok to cool to room temperature. The dish is then ready to be used for steaming. There is no need to repeat this process as it will remain tempered for its lifetime.

using a bamboo steamer

Bamboo steamers come in a range of sizes to fit any wok. For a standard 30–35 cm (12–14 inch) wok, look for steamer baskets about 25–32 cm (10–13 inches) in diameter. Buy at least two same-sized baskets and a lid so that you can stack them and cook a larger quantity of food in one go.

Before you use a bamboo steamer for the first time, immerse it in water for 15 minutes to get rid of the strong bamboo smell.

To stop food from sticking to the base of the steamer, either oil or line the steamer. The benefit of lining the steamer is that it prevents food from absorbing the bamboo smell. Both baking paper and banana leaves work well, with banana leaves having the advantage of being visually appealing.

Once the bamboo basket is lined and the food is in place, fit the lid on the steamer basket (you won't need the wok lid). Sit the basket over a wok of simmering water. Remember, if you are using layers of baskets, you will need to swap their positions halfway through the cooking time so that the food cooks evenly.

Although bamboo steamers are easy to maintain, they do need to be washed after each use and allowed to dry thoroughly before storing, especially after being used to cook strong-smelling food such as fish. If they are stored while still wet, they may become mildewed.

getting going

Fill the wok one-third full of boiling water, or use cold water and bring to the boil, then reduce the heat and keep it at a fast simmer. Don't be tempted to over-fill the wok, or the water will boil up into the food, spoiling it. But if you use too little it may boil dry.

The bottom of the steamer must not touch the water, otherwise the water will taint the food. If you are using a ceramic dish, make sure there is enough room around the side for you to remove it easily. If steaming for longer than 10 minutes, have extra boiling water ready to replenish during cooking.

Be careful when removing the lid. Always lift it up so that it forms a shield, preventing the steam from scalding you. Take care when removing any dish or food from the steamer as the steam can burn. Turn off the heat first then remove the food. Remove a dish using a tea towel or oven gloves.

Even when the steaming dish has been removed from the heat, the food will continue to cook for some time, so take care not to overcook it. Always remove cooked food from the steamer immediately or, if you are serving the food in the steamer, serve it straight away.

steaming techniques

Only fill a wok **one-third** full of boiling water.

Oil the base of the steamer to stop food **sticking**, or line it with baking paper or **banana leaves**.

Sit the food in the wok in a **single layer**.

If cooking large quantities of food, use **stacks** of steamers, covering the **top one** with the lid.

har gow dumplings

makes 24

filling

500 g (1 lb 2 oz) **raw prawns (shrimp)**, peeled and deveined

45 g (1 1/2 oz) **pork** or **bacon fat** (rind removed), finely diced

40 g (1 1/2 oz) finely chopped **bamboo shoots**

1 **spring onion (scallion)**, finely chopped

1 teaspoon **sugar**

3 teaspoons **soy sauce**

1/2 teaspoon **roasted sesame oil**

1 **egg white**, lightly beaten

1 teaspoon **salt**

1 tablespoon **cornflour (cornstarch)**

24 **gow gee wrappers** (8–9 cm/3 1/4–3 1/2 inches)

soy sauce or **hot chilli sauce**, to serve

Pleat the dumplings using your thumb and index finger.

Once pleated, carefully bring the two **opposite ends** together and **pinch** to seal.

To make the filling, cut half the prawns into 1 cm (1/2 inch) chunks, then chop the remaining prawns using a knife or food processor until finely minced. Combine all the prawns in a large bowl. Add the pork fat, bamboo shoots, spring onion, sugar, soy sauce, sesame oil, egg white, salt and cornflour. Mix well.

Put 1 teaspoon of the filling in the centre of each gow gee wrapper and fold the wrapper over to make a half-moon shape. Spread a little water along the edge of the wrapper and use your thumb and index finger to form small pleats along the outside edge. With the other hand, press the two opposite edges together to seal. The inside edge should curve in a semicircle to conform to the shape of the pleated edge.

Line two bamboo steamers with baking paper and punch with holes. Put the dumplings in the steamers and cover to prevent them drying out while you work.

When you are ready to cook the har gow, sit the steamers over a wok of simmering water and steam, covered, for 6–8 minutes, or until the wrappers are translucent. Reverse the steamers halfway through cooking. Serve with soy or hot chilli sauce.

tip Shaping the har gow takes a little practice — don't overfill them or the filling will leak out and they won't fold or stick properly.

steamed oysters with hot sesame oil

makes 24

rock salt, for lining

24 shucked **oysters**

3 **spring onions (scallions)**, trimmed and cut into 5 cm (2 inch) julienne strips

1 **long red chilli**, seeded and cut into very thin strips

3 teaspoons finely grated fresh **ginger**

1 tablespoon **light soy sauce**

1 tablespoon roughly chopped **coriander (cilantro) leaves** (optional)

1 tablespoon **sesame oil**

Fill a wok one-third full of water and bring to simmering point. Take a plate that fits in your steamer basket (with sufficient space around it for you to remove the plate when it is hot) and line the plate with rock salt.

Arrange a single layer of oysters on top of the salt — this will prevent them sliding around. Put some spring onion, chilli and ginger on each oyster and drizzle with a little soy sauce. Cover and steam over the wok of simmering water for 2 minutes. Repeat with the remaining oysters, scattering with a little coriander when steamed.

Put the sesame oil in a small saucepan and heat briefly over high heat. Drizzle the oil over the oysters and serve immediately.

steamed crab meat in ramekins

serves 4 as a starter

2 x 170 g (6 oz) tins **crab meat** (or 350 g/12 oz fresh)

300 g (10 1/2 oz) **white boneless fish fillets**, chopped

140 g (5 oz) tin **coconut milk**

1 stem **lemon grass**, white part only, finely chopped

2 **spring onions (scallions)**, finely chopped

1 tablespoon **fish sauce**

1 teaspoon **lime juice**

1 teaspoon grated **palm sugar**

2 **eggs**, separated

3 tablespoons chopped **coriander (cilantro) leaves**

4 **makrut (kaffir lime) leaves**

Drain the crab meat, then squeeze dry with your hands. Set aside.

Pat the fish pieces dry with paper towels and put in a food processor with the coconut milk, lemon grass, spring onion, fish sauce, lime juice, palm sugar and the egg yolks. Process until smooth, then transfer to a bowl and fold in the crab meat and coriander.

Beat the egg whites to soft peaks, then fold into the fish mixture. Spoon into four 185 ml (6 fl oz/3/4 cup) ramekins and smooth the surface. Top each ramekin with a lime leaf.

Evenly space the ramekins in a large bamboo steamer. Sit the steamer over a wok of simmering water and steam, covered, for 20 minutes, or until cooked through. Serve warm or cold.

open vegetarian dumplings

makes 15

8 **dried shiitake mushrooms**

3 **garlic cloves**, crushed

2 teaspoons grated fresh **ginger**

5 **spring onions (scallions)**, finely chopped

60 g (2¼ oz/¼ bunch) **water spinach (ong choy)**, chopped

60 g (2¼ oz/⅓ cup) diced **water chestnuts**

40 g (1½ oz/¼ cup) toasted **unsalted peanuts**, chopped

3 tablespoons chopped **coriander (cilantro) leaves and stems**

2 teaspoons **Chinese rice wine**

2 tablespoons **kecap manis**

1 teaspoon **sesame oil**

15 round **won ton wrappers**

4 tablespoons **sweet plum sauce** (see tip)

Soak the shiitake mushrooms in boiling water for 5 minutes, or until softened. Drain, discard the woody stems and finely chop the caps. Transfer to a bowl with the garlic, ginger, spring onion, water spinach, water chestnuts, peanuts, coriander, rice wine, kecap manis and sesame oil and stir until well combined.

Put 1 tablespoon of the mixture in the centre of a won ton wrapper, and lightly brush the edges with water. Bring the edges up around the filling, pleating as you go to encase the filling. The top should be open. Repeat with the remaining wrappers and filling to make 15 dumplings.

Line a large 30 cm (12 inch) bamboo steamer with baking paper and punch with holes. Arrange the dumplings on top in a single layer. Sit the steamer over a wok of simmering water and steam, covered, for 5 minutes, or until cooked through. If you don't have a large steamer, cook the dumplings in batches or use two smaller steamers, swapping them halfway through. Serve with the plum sauce.

tip The sweet plum sauce comes in a similar bottle to sweet chilli sauce and is fairly light in colour. It is not the same as plum sauce sold in western-style supermarkets. Look for it in Asian food shops.

steamed thai fish cakes

makes 24

chilli lime dipping sauce

1 small **red chilli**, seeded and finely chopped

1 teaspoon **caster (superfine) sugar**

1 1/2 tablespoons **rice vinegar**

1 1/2 tablespoons **lime juice**

2 tablespoons **fish sauce**

1/4 small **carrot**, finely chopped

1/4 small **Lebanese (short) cucumber**,
   seeded and finely chopped

600 g (1 lb 5 oz) **firm, skinless white fish fillets**
   (such as ling, bream or redfish)

2 tablespoons **red curry paste**

2 tablespoons **fish sauce**

3 teaspoons **lime juice**

1 **egg**, lightly beaten

2 tablespoons finely chopped **coriander (cilantro)
   leaves and roots**

4 **makrut (kaffir lime) leaves**, finely chopped

150 g (5 1/2 oz) **snake beans**, finely chopped

24 **mint leaves**

To make the dipping sauce, combine all the ingredients and 3 tablespoons of water in a bowl and stir until the sugar dissolves and the ingredients are well combined.

Put the fish, curry paste, fish sauce and lime juice in a food processor and process until a smooth, sticky paste is formed. Transfer to a large non-metallic bowl and add the egg, coriander, lime leaves, snake beans and 1/2 teaspoon of salt. Using your hands, mix until the ingredients are well combined.

Line a large bamboo steamer with baking paper and punch with holes. Shape tablespoons of the fish mixture into 24 small balls, then flatten gently with the palm of your hand to form patties. Arrange the patties in the steamer, making sure they don't touch each other (use a second bamboo steamer if necessary). Put a mint leaf on top of each patty. Sit the steamer over a wok of simmering water and steam, covered, for 10–12 minutes, or until cooked through. Remove from the heat and serve immediately with the chilli lime dipping sauce.

The **easiest way** to seed a cucumber is using **a teaspoon**.

Make sure all the **ingredients** are well combined.

steamed prawns with coriander and green mango salad

serves 4 as a starter

dressing

2 teaspoons **lime juice**

1 tablespoon **fish sauce**

1 **garlic clove**, crushed

1/2 teaspoon **rice vinegar**

1/2 teaspoon **soft brown sugar**

2 tablespoons **fresh coconut juice** or
2 teaspoons **coconut milk** mixed
with 1 1/2 tablespoons water (see tip)

12 large **raw prawns (shrimp)**, peeled
and deveined, tails removed

1 large **red chilli**, seeded and thinly
shredded

3 **red Asian shallots**, finely sliced

1 large **green mango**, peeled and
shredded (see tip)

1 large handful **coriander (cilantro)
leaves**

2 **makrut (kaffir lime) leaves**,
shredded

To make the dressing, combine the lime juice, fish sauce, garlic, vinegar, sugar and coconut juice in a bowl.

Line a bamboo steamer with baking paper and punch with holes. Arrange the prawns in a single layer in the steamer. Sit the steamer over a wok of simmering water and steam, covered, for 3–4 minutes, or until the prawns turn opaque.

Combine the chilli, shallots, mango, coriander and lime leaves in a bowl. Add the prawns to the salad, drizzle on the dressing and toss gently to coat. Serve at once or at room temperature.

tips Fresh coconut juice is not the same as coconut milk. The juice is the liquid found inside the coconut, whereas coconut milk and cream are extracted from the coconut flesh. Coconut juice and green mangoes can be found in Asian food stores and larger general supermarkets.

chinese duck dumplings

makes 30

filling

300 g (10½ oz) **duck breast fillet**, skin removed

2 teaspoons finely grated fresh **ginger**

2 **garlic cloves**, finely chopped

½ teaspoon **ground ginger**

¼ teaspoon **five-spice powder**

¼ teaspoon ground **white pepper**

1½ tablespoons **plum sauce**

1 tablespoon **Chinese rice wine**

2 teaspoons **light soy sauce**

sesame oil, for drizzling

40 g (1½ oz/¼ cup) **water chestnuts**, finely chopped

1 tablespoon finely snipped **garlic chives**

30 square **won ton wrappers**

vegetable oil, for shallow-frying

400 ml (14 fl oz) **chicken stock**

Chinese red vinegar, to serve

light soy sauce, to serve

Bring up **the corners** to meet in the middle, sealing along the **edges**.

Cook the **dumplings in batches** so you don't overcrowd the wok.

338

To make the filling, combine the duck, ginger, garlic, ground ginger, five-spice powder, white pepper, plum sauce, rice wine, soy sauce, 1/2 teaspoon of salt and a few drops of sesame oil in a food processor and process until well combined and the duck is minced. Transfer to a non-metallic bowl and stir in the water chestnuts and garlic chives. Cover and refrigerate for 2 hours to allow the flavours to develop.

Put 2 heaped teaspoons of the mixture in the centre of a won ton wrapper, lightly moisten the edges with water and bring up two diagonal edges of the wrapper to join together and seal. Repeat with the other two corners. Pinch along the seams to seal. Repeat with the remaining filling and wrappers to make 30 dumplings.

Heat 1 tablespoon of oil in a large wok over medium heat. Add the dumplings in batches flat-side-down and cook for 2 minutes, or until just brown on the bottom. Add 3 tablespoons of stock for each batch, then quickly cover with a lid as they may spit. Steam for 2–3 minutes, taking care that all the stock doesn't evaporate and the dumplings do not burn. Serve hot with the Chinese red vinegar and soy sauce for dipping.

steamed scallops with lime sauce

serves 4 as a starter

lime sauce

1 teaspoon **soft brown sugar**

2 tablespoons **lime juice**

1/4 teaspoon **chilli sauce**

1 tablespoon **sweet soy sauce**

12 **scallops** in the half shell

2 small **makrut (kaffir lime) leaves**, shredded

12 **Thai basil** or **holy basil leaves**, torn

1 small **red chilli**, seeded and thinly sliced

To make the lime sauce, combine the sugar, lime juice, chilli sauce and sweet soy sauce in a small bowl.

Fill a large wok one-third full of water, bring to the boil then reduce to a simmer. Cover with a bamboo steamer and arrange four of the scallops in their shells in the steamer. Cover and steam for 2–3 minutes, or until the scallops are opaque but still plump (the time will depend on their plumpness). Remove with tongs and steam the remaining scallops. As each batch is taken out, add the juices from the scallop shells to the lime sauce.

Arrange three shells on each serving plate. Spoon a little sauce over the scallops and top with the lime and basil leaves and the chilli. Serve warm or chilled.

lemper

makes 20

coconut rice

500 g (1 lb 2 oz/2½ cups) **glutinous white rice**,
   soaked in cold water for 30 minutes
250 ml (9 fl oz/1 cup) **coconut cream**

filling

2 tablespoons **peanut oil**
1 small **red chilli**, seeded and finely chopped
4 **garlic cloves**, finely chopped
3–4 **red Asian shallots**, finely chopped
1 stem **lemon grass**, white part only, finely chopped
4 fresh **curry leaves**, crushed
2 teaspoons **ground coriander**
2 teaspoons **ground cumin**
1 teaspoon **dried shrimp paste**
300 g (10½ oz) **minced (ground) chicken**
white pepper, to taste
2 teaspoons **lemon juice**
2 **banana leaves** (see tip)

To make the coconut rice, rinse the rice several times under cold running water. Put the rice and 500 ml (17 fl oz/2 cups) of water in a large saucepan, bring to the boil and cover with a tight-fitting lid. Reduce the heat and simmer for 15 minutes. Add 185 ml (6 fl oz/3/4 cup) of the coconut cream and 125 ml (4 fl oz/1/2 cup) of water and stir well. Cover and continue to cook over very low heat for 5–10 minutes, or until the liquid is absorbed. Remove from the heat and leave with the lid on for about 10 minutes.

To make the filling, heat a wok over medium heat, add the oil and swirl to coat. Add the chilli, garlic, shallots, lemon grass and curry leaves and stir-fry for 1 minute, or until fragrant. Add the coriander, cumin and shrimp paste, and cook for another minute, stirring in the shrimp paste until it is well combined. Add the chicken and stir-fry for 3 minutes, or until it changes colour. Pour in the remaining coconut cream and cook over low heat for 8–10 minutes, or until the mixture is quite dry. Season with salt and white pepper to taste and drizzle with the lemon juice. Spread out on a lined baking tray until cool. Divide into 20 portions.

Wash the banana leaves in warm water. Cut them down the centre to remove the rib, then cut into 14 x 8 cm (51/2 x 31/4 inch) rectangles. You may need to soak them in hot water to make them pliable, but make sure they are dry before using them to wrap the rice. Spread a portion of rice to 1 cm (1/2 inch) thick over each rectangle, leaving a 5 mm (1/4 inch) border on each end. Put 1 tablespoon of the chicken mixture in the centre of the rice and roll into a cylinder, securing with kitchen string or a toothpick.

Put a single layer of lemper seam-side-down in a bamboo steamer. Sit the steamer over a wok of simmering water and steam for 5 minutes. Repeat with the remaining lemper. Alternatively, use stacks of steamers, swap them halfway through and cook for 1–2 minutes longer. Serve at room temperature.

tip You can use greaseproof baking paper or heavy-duty foil to wrap the rice if banana leaves are unavailable.

Carefully roll up **the banana leaves** to wrap the filling.

Only put a **single layer** of the lemper in each steamer.

steamed prawn and noodle salad

serves 4

2 tablespoons **Chinese rice wine**

pinch of **sugar**

1 tablespoon **fish sauce**

20 **raw king prawns (shrimp)**, peeled and deveined,
   tails removed

90 g (3¼ oz/1 bunch) **coriander (cilantro)**

80 g (2¾ oz/1 bunch) **mint**

200 g (7 oz) **dried rice vermicelli**

4 tablespoons **lime juice**

4 tablespoons **peanut** or **vegetable oil**

1 teaspoon **sesame oil**

5 cm (2 inch) piece fresh **ginger**, thinly sliced on the diagonal

Toss the salad

thoroughly so the noodles

are well flavoured.

The fresh coriander and mint

leaves will add a **subtle**

flavour to the prawns.

Combine the rice wine, sugar and fish sauce in a bowl. Add the prawns and toss them through the mixture. Cover and leave to marinate for 10 minutes.

Divide the bunch of coriander in two and set aside one half. Finely chop half of the remaining coriander and pick the whole leaves from the stems that are left (reserve these for the garnish). Repeat with the bunch of mint.

Cook the vermicelli according to the packet instructions. Drain well and put in a large bowl. Add the lime juice, peanut oil, sesame oil and the chopped coriander and mint. Season with salt and black pepper and toss well.

Put a shallow heatproof bowl inside a bamboo steamer and line it with the ginger slices and the reserved half bunches of coriander and mint. Sit the prawns and any liquid on the herbs and steam over a wok of simmering water for 4–5 minutes, or until the prawns are pink and cooked through. Carefully remove the bowl from the steamer.

Divide the vermicelli among four serving plates. Top with the prawns and the cooking juices and garnish with the whole coriander and mint leaves.

steamed tofu with mirin dressing

serves 4 as part of a spread

300 g (10 1/2 oz) **silken firm tofu**

2 tablespoons **sake**

2 tablespoons **mirin**

2 tablespoons **soy sauce**

3 **spring onions (scallions)**

2 cm (3/4 inch) piece fresh **ginger**, julienned

mirin dressing

3 tablespoons **dashi granules**

1 tablespoon **mirin**

1 teaspoon **Japanese soy sauce**

Carefully slice the tofu into eight equal pieces and put on a lipped plate that will fit inside a bamboo steamer. Combine the sake, mirin and soy sauce and pour over the tofu. Cover and marinate, turning once, for 30 minutes.

Slice the whites of the spring onions on the diagonal and finely slice the green part of two of the spring onions on the diagonal.

Put the plate of tofu in the steamer and sit the steamer over a wok of simmering water. Scatter the ginger and white spring onion slices over the tofu, then steam, covered, for 5 minutes.

To make the dressing, combine the dashi granules with 3 tablespoons of water. Add the mirin and soy sauce and mix well.

Arrange the tofu on a serving plate, drizzle with the dressing and scatter the spring onion greens on top. Serve warm.

sticky rice and pork pockets

makes 8

600 g (1 lb 5 oz/3 cups) **glutinous white rice**

4 large **lotus leaves** (see tip)

4 **dried Chinese mushrooms**

2 tablespoons **dried shrimp**

350 g (12 oz) **pork leg** or **loin fillet**, cut into 4 cm (1½ inch) cubes

2 teaspoons finely sliced fresh **ginger**

1½ tablespoons **soy sauce**

1½ tablespoons **cornflour (cornstarch)**

1 tablespoon **oyster sauce**

2 teaspoons **sugar**

1 teaspoon **sesame oil**

2 tablespoons **vegetable oil**

1 **garlic clove**, finely chopped

2 **Chinese sausages (lap cheong)**, thinly sliced

2 **spring onions (scallions)**, finely sliced

Wash the rice under cold running water, drain well and put in a saucepan with 625 ml (22 fl oz/2 1/2 cups) of water. Bring to the boil over high heat, then reduce the heat to low, cover with a tight-fitting lid and simmer for 20 minutes. Allow to cool. Cut the lotus leaves in half to give eight equal-sized pieces. Put the lotus leaves in a large bowl and cover with boiling water for 1 hour. Pat dry with paper towels.

Meanwhile, put the dried mushrooms and dried shrimp in separate bowls, cover each with boiling water and soak for 15–20 minutes. Drain well. Remove the stems from the mushrooms and finely chop the caps. Finely chop the shrimp. Put the pork in a food processor and briefly pulse to a very coarse texture. Transfer the pork to a bowl, add the ginger, 1 tablespoon of soy sauce and 2 teaspoons of cornflour, and toss well. Leave the pork to marinate for 20–30 minutes. Combine the oyster sauce, sugar, sesame oil and remaining soy sauce in a bowl and stir to combine.

Heat a wok over high heat, add the vegetable oil and swirl to coat. When hot, add the pork and cook for 2–3 minutes, stirring constantly. Add the garlic, sausage, spring onion, mushroom and shrimp and stir-fry for 2 minutes. Add the soy and oyster sauce mixture and toss well. Combine the remaining cornflour with 200 ml (7 fl oz) of water, gradually add to the wok and stir for 1 minute, or until the pork mixture has thickened.

With wet hands, roll and shape the cooked rice into 16 equal-sized balls. With the ribs on the inside, fold one end of a lotus leaf piece on the diagonal to form a cone. Hold securely in one hand and spoon in a ball of rice. Make an indent in the centre of the rice, spoon one-eighth of the pork mixture into the middle of the rice, then top with another rice ball. Fold the other end of the lotus leaf over to enclose the filling, then secure with a toothpick. Tie tightly with kitchen string if necessary. The parcel should be triangular. Repeat with the remaining lotus leaves, rice balls and filling to make eight parcels.

Arrange the rice parcels in a single layer in a double bamboo steamer. Sit the steamers over a wok of simmering water and steam, covered, for 15 minutes. Reverse the steamers and steam for a further 15 minutes, adding more hot water to the wok as necessary. Serve immediately.

tip Look for lotus leaves in Asian supermarkets. They are large dried leaves, often about 60 cm (24 inches) in diameter, and come folded. They need to be soaked before you use them.

With the lotus leaf in a **cone shape**, carefully insert a rice ball.

To keep the **parcels closed** during steaming, secure with a **toothpick**.

steamed mud crab with spicy tamarind sauce

serves 4

2 small **mud crabs**, about 1.25 kg
(2 lb 12 oz) in total

2 stems **lemon grass**, outer leaves
discarded, bruised

4 **spring onions (scallions)**, trimmed

3 cm (1 1/4 inch) piece fresh **ginger**,
sliced lengthways

spicy tamarind sauce

2 tablespoons **vegetable oil**

3 **garlic cloves**, crushed

1/2 teaspoon **white peppercorns**,
crushed

3 tablespoons **fish sauce**

2 teaspoons **sambal oelek**

1 tablespoon **tamarind paste**

3 tablespoons **Chinese rice wine**

Kill the mud crabs humanely by putting them in the freezer for 2 hours. Using a heavy cleaver, chop each into four pieces. Remove the soft internal organs and the roe, and rinse the cavities clean.

Line a bamboo steamer with baking paper and punch with holes. Arrange the lemon grass, spring onion and ginger slices on top in a single layer. Top with a single layer of the crab sections (the steaming may have to be done in batches). Sit the steamer over a wok of simmering water and steam, covered, for 12–15 minutes per batch, or until the flesh is cooked and the shells are bright red.

To make the sauce, heat the oil in a small saucepan over medium heat and add the garlic and peppercorns. When the garlic starts to brown, add the fish sauce, sambal oelek, tamarind, rice wine and 3 tablespoons of water. Simmer for 2 minutes, then remove and keep warm until ready to serve.

To serve, pile the crab on a serving platter and pour the sauce over the top.

tip Although steamed rice is the traditional accompaniment, crusty bread is great for soaking up the sauce.

steamed chicken on wilted greens with ginger and shallot dressing

serves 4

ginger and shallot dressing

2 x 2 cm (3/4 x 3/4 inch) piece fresh **ginger**, julienned

125 ml (4 fl oz/1/2 cup) **soy sauce**

2 tablespoons **Chinese rice wine**

1 **garlic clove**, crushed

1/2 teaspoon **sesame oil**

1 tablespoon finely chopped **coriander (cilantro) stems**

4 **spring onions (scallions)**, thinly sliced on the diagonal

6 **makrut (kaffir lime) leaves**, crushed

1 stem **lemon grass**, cut into thirds and bruised

4 x 4 cm (11/2 x 11/2 inch) piece fresh **ginger**, sliced

10 g (1/4 oz) **dried shiitake mushrooms**

4 **chicken breast fillets**

700 g (1 lb 9 oz/1 bunch) **Chinese broccoli (gai lan)**, trimmed and cut into thirds

4 tablespoons **coriander (cilantro) leaves**

To make the dressing, combine all the ingredients in a bowl.

Fill a wok one-third full of water, add the lime leaves, lemon grass, ginger and mushrooms and bring to the boil over high heat. Reduce the heat to a simmer. Line a large bamboo steamer with baking paper and punch with holes. Arrange the chicken fillets on top. Sit the steamer over the wok of simmering water and steam, covered, for 10 minutes, or until the chicken is cooked. Remove and keep warm. Add the Chinese broccoli to the steamer and steam, covered, for 2–3 minutes, or until just wilted. Remove and keep warm.

Strain the steaming liquid through a sieve, reserving the liquid and the mushrooms. Remove the stems from the mushrooms and discard. Thinly slice the caps and add them to the dressing with 125 ml (4 fl oz/1/2 cup) of the reserved liquid. Cut each chicken breast into three pieces on the diagonal. Divide the Chinese broccoli among four serving plates, top with the chicken and spoon the dressing over the top. Garnish with the coriander and serve immediately.

steamed pork ribs in black bean sauce

serves 4 as part of a spread

400 g (14 oz) **American-style pork ribs**, chopped into individual ribs about 8 cm (31/4 inches) long (ask your butcher to do this if you do not have a cleaver)

11/2 tablespoons **black beans**, washed and slightly mashed with a fork

2 **garlic cloves**, chopped

1 cm (1/2 inch) piece fresh **ginger**, finely chopped

1 tablespoon **oyster sauce**

2 teaspoons **soy sauce**

2 teaspoons **sugar**

1 tablespoon **cornflour (cornstarch)**

1 **spring onion (scallion)**, cut into 2 cm (3/4 inch) lengths

Put the chopped ribs in a shallow heatproof dish that will fit into a bamboo steamer. Combine the black beans, garlic, ginger, oyster sauce, soy sauce and sugar in a small bowl and mix well. Stir in the cornflour. Add the mixture to the ribs and mix well with clean hands. Scatter the spring onion over the top.

Put the dish in the steamer and sit the steamer over a wok of boiling water. Steam, covered, for 20 minutes (replenish the water if necessary during steaming). During cooking the steam will create a sauce for the ribs. Serve hot with steamed rice and a vegetable side dish.

tip Make sure the lid is tight fitting as you need a lot of steam to help create the sauce; if necessary, add 1–2 tablespoons of boiling water to the dish.

marinated steamed salmon

serves 4

10 cm (4 inch) piece **lemon grass**

5 cm (2 inch) piece fresh **ginger**, finely grated

2 tablespoons **sweet chilli sauce**

1 small **red chilli**, seeded and finely chopped

1 tablespoon **fish sauce**

2 tablespoons **lime juice**

1 tablespoon **vegetable oil**

4 tablespoons chopped **coriander (cilantro) leaves**

4 x 180 g (6 oz) **salmon fillets**

2 **spring onions (scallions)**, finely chopped

Remove the outer layers of the lemon grass and finely chop the rest. Combine in a bowl with the ginger, sweet chilli sauce, chilli, fish sauce, lime juice, oil and 2 tablespoons of the coriander. Mix well using a fork.

Put the salmon in a shallow non-metallic dish and pour the marinade over the top. Cover and refrigerate for 1 hour, then remove from the marinade, allowing any excess to drip off.

Line a bamboo steamer with baking paper and punch with holes. Arrange the salmon fillets on top in a single layer. Sit the steamer over a wok of simmering water, making sure the bottom of the steamer doesn't touch the water, and steam, covered, for 10–12 minutes, depending on how well you want the salmon cooked.

Combine the remaining coriander with the spring onion and scatter over the salmon before serving.

fish in spiced nut sauce

serves 4

16 **almonds**

2 cm (3/4 inch) piece fresh **ginger**, roughly chopped

2–3 **red bird's eye chillies**, seeded

5 **red Asian shallots**, roughly chopped

2 **garlic cloves**

1 large **Roma (plum) tomato** or 2 medium ones, roughly chopped

2 teaspoons **fish sauce**

2 teaspoons **palm sugar** or **soft brown sugar**

2 **spring onions (scallions)**, sliced

4 x 180 g (6 oz) **white fish fillets** (such as perch, barramundi or snapper)

banana leaves, blanched, to wrap (see tip)

lemon or **lime wedges**, to serve

Heat a frying pan over high heat. Add the almonds and dry-fry for 4–5 minutes. Cool. Put the almonds, ginger, chillies, shallots, garlic, tomato and 1/2 teaspoon of salt in a small food processor or blender and process until smooth. Stir in the fish sauce, sugar and half the spring onion.

Spread the paste over the fish fillets. Cut out four pieces of banana leaf large enough to enclose the fish. Sit the fish in the middle of the leaves, fold in the sides and roll over to tightly enclose in the leaves.

Put the fish parcels in a bamboo steamer. Sit the steamer over a wok of simmering water and steam, covered, for 7–8 minutes, or until the fish flakes when tested. Remove from the parcels and garnish with the remaining spring onion. Serve with lemon or lime wedges and steamed rice.

tip If you prefer, you can use a large sheet of greased aluminium foil instead of banana leaves to wrap the fish.

chinese steamed rice parcels

makes 4

2 **lotus leaves**

6 **dried shiitake mushrooms**

275 g (9¾ oz/1¼ cups) **short-grain rice**

1 tablespoon **peanut oil**

250 g (9 oz) **chicken thigh fillets**, cut into 1.5 cm (⅝ inch) cubes

2 **garlic cloves**, crushed

3 teaspoons grated fresh **ginger**

60 g (2¼ oz/⅓ cup) finely diced **water chestnuts**

1 tablespoon **Chinese rice wine**

3 tablespoons **chicken stock**

3 tablespoons **light soy sauce**

4 **spring onions (scallions)**, thinly sliced

1 teaspoon **cornflour (cornstarch)**

Once the rice has been added **stir everything** well until combined.

Fold up the **bottom edge** first, then fold in the sides. **Flip over** to completely enclose the filling.

Cut each lotus leaf in half, then soak in hot water for 1 hour. Pat dry with paper towels.

Soak the shiitake mushrooms in 250 ml (9 fl oz/1 cup) of boiling water for about 20 minutes, then drain, reserving the soaking liquid. Remove the stems and thinly slice the caps.

Rinse the rice and put in a saucepan with 375 ml (13 fl oz/1 1/2 cups) of water. Bring to the boil, then reduce the heat to low and cook, covered, for 10 minutes. Remove from the heat and leave, covered, for another 10 minutes.

Heat the oil in a wok, add the chicken and cook for 3 minutes, or until browned. Add the garlic, ginger, water chestnuts and sliced mushroom and cook for another 30 seconds. Stir in the rice wine, chicken stock, 2 tablespoons of soy sauce, the spring onion and 3 tablespoons of the shiitake soaking liquid. Mix the cornflour with 1 tablespoon of water, add to the wok and cook until the mixture thickens. Stir in the rice and the remaining soy sauce and mix well.

Remove the lotus leaves from the water. Put one-quarter of the rice mixture in the centre of each leaf, making a mound about 8 x 6 cm (3 1/4 x 2 1/2 inches). Fold up the bottom edge, fold in the short sides, then flip the parcel up to completely enclose the filling. Repeat with the remaining mixture and leaves to make four parcels.

Put the parcels, seam-side-down, in a large bamboo steamer. Sit the steamer over a wok of simmering water and steam, covered, for 20 minutes. Serve hot.

tip The parcels can be unwrapped and served as part of a spread or eaten individually, warm or cold, as a light meal. For smaller parcels, the lotus leaves can be cut into quarters.

steamed chicken with chinese vegetables

serves 4

5 cm (2 inch) piece fresh **ginger**, finely grated

2 **garlic cloves**, crushed

1 tablespoon finely chopped **coriander (cilantro) root**

2 tablespoons **lime juice**

1 teaspoon **sesame oil**

3 tablespoons **soy sauce**

500 g (1 lb 2 oz) **chicken breast fillet**, thinly sliced

100 g (3 1/2 oz) fresh **shiitake mushrooms**, sliced

125 g (4 1/2 oz) other **Chinese mushrooms**
   (such as enoki, oyster or black fungus), torn

125 g (4 1/2 oz) **baby corn**, halved lengthways

coriander (cilantro) leaves, to serve

Combine the ginger, garlic, coriander root, lime juice, oil and soy sauce in a small bowl or jug.

Put the chicken strips in a heatproof shallow dish that fits into a large bamboo steamer. Spoon on half the sauce and toss the chicken to coat it in the sauce. Top with the mushrooms and baby corn. Put the dish in the steamer basket and pour on the remaining sauce.

Sit the steamer over a wok of simmering water and steam, covered, for 25 minutes, or until the chicken is cooked through. Garnish with coriander leaves and serve with boiled or steamed rice.

steamed pork and crab curry in banana leaves

makes 4

2 **banana leaves**

200 g (7 oz) **minced (ground) pork**

175 g (6 oz) tin **crab meat**, drained and squeezed dry

3 **spring onions (scallions)**, finely chopped

2 tablespoons chopped **Thai basil leaves**

1 **egg**, lightly beaten

270 ml (9½ fl oz) tin **coconut cream**

1–1½ teaspoons **red curry paste**

2 teaspoons **fish sauce**

1 **garlic clove**, crushed

1 teaspoon grated fresh **ginger**

4 **Thai basil leaves**, extra, to serve

Cut the banana leaves into eight 14 cm (5½ inch) squares. Blanch the squares briefly in boiling water to soften. Put two squares together. Cut a 5 cm (2 inch) incision from each corner towards the centre, then fold in the corners, securing with a toothpick (or staple) to form a double basket. Line a large bamboo steamer with the remaining banana leaf scraps.

Put the pork, crab meat, spring onion, basil and beaten egg in a bowl and mix together well. Reserve 2 tablespoons of coconut cream for later, then combine the remaining coconut cream, the curry paste, fish sauce, garlic and ginger in a small bowl. Add to the pork mixture and mix well.

Put the banana baskets in the steamer, then spoon the pork and crab mixture into the baskets. Top with a spoonful of the reserved coconut cream. Sit the steamer over a wok of simmering water and steam, covered, for 25 minutes, or until cooked through. Serve immediately, garnished with a basil leaf.

steamed snapper with ginger and shallots

serves 4 as part of a spread

6 **spring onions (scallions)**, sliced on the diagonal

2 small (400 g/14 oz each) **whole snapper**, cleaned and scaled

2 teaspoons **salt**

2 teaspoons **sesame oil**

3 tablespoons **light soy sauce**

3 tablespoons julienned fresh **ginger**

60 g (21/4 oz) fresh **shiitake mushrooms**, sliced

2 tablespoons **peanut oil**

11/2 tablespoons **Chinese rice wine**

coriander (cilantro) sprigs (optional), to serve

Lightly oil two plates large enough to hold each fish and sit them in two layers of a bamboo steamer. Take half the spring onions and divide between the two plates. Pat the fish dry with paper towels, then lay the fish on top of the spring onion. Combine the salt, sesame oil and 2 tablespoons of soy sauce and rub the mixture over each fish. Scatter the ginger and mushrooms over the fish, putting some in each cavity.

Sit the steamers over a wok of simmering water and steam, covered, for 30 minutes, or until the fish is just cooked through. Swap the steamers over halfway through cooking. Remove the plates from the steamer.

Heat the peanut oil in a small saucepan over medium heat until it starts to smoke — the oil must be hot enough to crisp the skin of the fish, otherwise it will taste oily. Drizzle the rice wine and remaining soy sauce evenly over the fish, then scatter with the remaining spring onion. Gently pour the hot oil over the whole length of the fish (take care as it will sizzle and splatter). Serve immediately, garnished with the coriander sprigs.

steamed salmon with snowpeas, asparagus and citrus butter

serves 4

citrus butter

1 **orange**

80 g (2³/4 oz) **butter**, softened

1 tablespoon **chervil**, chopped

250 g (9 oz) **snowpeas (mangetout)**, topped and tailed

350 g (12 oz/2 bunches) **asparagus**, trimmed and halved (see tip)

4 x 180 g (6 oz) **salmon fillets**

To make the citrus butter, finely grate 2 teaspoons of the zest from the orange and squeeze 2 tablespoons of juice from one orange half. Put the butter in a bowl and gradually beat or whisk in the orange zest and juice. Add the chervil, season with salt and pepper and mix again. Chill in the refrigerator until needed.

Cut the remaining orange half into slices, then halve each slice. Line a bamboo steamer with baking paper and punch with holes. Put the snowpeas and asparagus in the steamer and arrange the orange slices on top. Sit the salmon fillets on top of the orange slices and season with salt and ground black pepper. Sit the steamer over a wok of simmering water, making sure the bottom of the steamer doesn't touch the water, and steam, covered, for 10–12 minutes, depending on how well you want the salmon cooked.

To serve, divide the vegetables among four warm serving plates (discarding the orange slices) and top each with a piece of salmon. Spread the citrus butter over the fish and vegetables and allow it to melt for a few seconds before serving.

tip If fresh asparagus is unavailable, buy 350 g (12 oz) zucchini (courgettes) instead. Cut them in half lengthways and then cut into 1 cm (½ inch) slices.

chicken with moroccan spices

serves 4

4 **chicken breast fillets**

chermoula

2 **garlic cloves**, crushed

2 **spring onions (scallions)**, white
  part only, finely chopped

2 tablespoons chopped **coriander
  (cilantro) leaves**

3 tablespoons **lemon juice**

2 tablespoons **olive oil**

1 teaspoon **ground cumin**

1 teaspoon **ground coriander**

1/2 teaspoon **hot paprika**

1/2 teaspoon **chilli powder**

couscous

200 g (7 oz) **couscous**

4 tablespoons **olive oil**

4 tablespoons **lemon juice**

55 g (2 oz/1/4 cup) pitted **green olives**,
  finely chopped

45 g (11/2 oz/1/2 cup) toasted **flaked
  almonds**

85 g (3 oz/2/3 cup) **sultanas**

4 tablespoons chopped **flat-leaf
  (Italian) parsley**

3 tablespoons chopped **coriander
  (cilantro) leaves**

Cut three slashes across the top of each chicken breast no more than 1 cm (1/2 inch) deep and put them in a shallow dish. Combine all the chermoula ingredients and pour over the chicken, turning the breasts over to ensure they are evenly coated. Leave to marinate in the refrigerator for at least 1 hour and up to 24 hours.

To make the couscous, put 250 ml (9 fl oz/1 cup) of water in a large saucepan with 2 tablespoons of oil and 1/2 teaspoon of salt. Bring to the boil, then add the couscous. Remove from the heat, cover and leave for about 3 minutes, or until it starts to swell. Return the saucepan to a very low heat for 3 minutes while fluffing up the grains with a fork. Transfer to a bowl and leave to cool for 5 minutes. Stir in the remaining ingredients and season well with salt and pepper.

Remove the chicken breasts from the chermoula, allowing any excess to drip off. Line a bamboo steamer with baking paper and punch with holes. Arrange the chicken on top in a single layer. Sit the steamer over a wok of simmering water, making sure the bottom of the steamer doesn't touch the water, and steam, covered, for 15 minutes, or until the chicken is cooked through. Serve the chicken with the couscous.

steamed chicken and fennel with salsa verde

serves 4

1 large **fennel bulb** (about 500 g/1 lb 2 oz), thinly sliced

1/2 small **lemon**, thinly sliced

4 **chicken breast fillets**

salsa verde

3 tablespoons finely chopped **flat-leaf (Italian) parsley**

3 tablespoons **baby capers**

1 large **garlic clove**, finely chopped

3 tablespoons **olive oil**

2 teaspoons finely grated **lemon zest**

2 tablespoons **lemon juice**

Line a large bamboo steamer with baking paper and punch with holes. Arrange the slices of fennel and lemon in the steamer and sit the chicken breasts on top. Season with salt and black pepper. Sit the steamer over a wok of simmering water, making sure the bottom of the steamer doesn't touch the water, and steam, covered, for about 15 minutes, or until the chicken is cooked through.

To make the salsa verde, combine all the ingredients in a bowl.

Serve the chicken with the salsa verde and the slices of fennel.

steamed coconut caramel custards

makes 4

175 g (6 oz/3/4 cup) **caster (superfine) sugar**
fresh fruit and **cream**, to serve

custard
4 **eggs**, lightly beaten
55 g (2 oz/1/4 cup) **caster (superfine) sugar**
400 ml (14 fl oz) tin **coconut cream**
30 g (1 oz/1/3 cup) **desiccated coconut**, lightly toasted

Combine the sugar and 250 ml (9 fl oz/1 cup) of water in a small saucepan. Stir over low heat until the sugar dissolves, then bring to the boil. Cook without stirring for 10–12 minutes, or until the mixture turns lightly golden. Remove from the heat and pour the caramel into four 250 ml (9 fl oz/1 cup) ramekins. Working quickly, gently tilt to coat the base and sides. Be careful as the ramekins will get hot.

To make the custard, combine the egg, sugar, coconut cream and desiccated coconut. Strain through a fine sieve, then divide the custard among the caramel-coated ramekins. Cover each with foil.

Put the ramekins in a bamboo steamer. Sit the steamer over a wok of simmering water and steam, covered, for 20–25 minutes, or until the custard is set. Alternatively, put a wire rack in a wok and pour in boiling water to just below the rack. Sit the ramekins on top, cover with a lid or sheet of foil and steam for 20–25 minutes.

Allow to cool, then put the custards in the refrigerator for at least 2 hours or overnight. Before serving, run a blunt knife around the edge and flip out onto a serving plate. Serve with fresh fruit and cream.

tip Allow about 125 ml (4 fl oz/1/2 cup) of custard per serve.

malay gow

makes 4 individual cakes or 1 large cake

2 **eggs**

95 g (3 1/4 oz/1/2 cup firmly packed) **soft brown sugar**

4 tablespoons **evaporated milk**

60 g (2 1/4 oz) **butter**, melted

90 g (3 1/4 oz/3/4 cup) **self-raising flour**

1/2 teaspoon **bicarbonate of soda**

maple syrup, to serve (optional)

whipped cream, to serve (optional)

Lightly grease and line the bases of four 250 ml (9 fl oz/1 cup) ramekins or one 20 cm (8 inch) cake tin.

Put the eggs and sugar in a small bowl and beat with an electric mixer for about 5 minutes, or until thick. Stir in the evaporated milk and melted butter. Fold in the flour and bicarbonate of soda. Divide the mixture evenly among the ramekins or pour into the cake tin.

Arrange the ramekins in a bamboo steamer. Sit the steamer over a wok of boiling water and steam, covered, for 20–25 minutes, or until cooked through. If making one large cake, cover the tin with foil and put on a steaming rack in the wok. Steam for 35–40 minutes, or until cooked.

These cakes are best served warm, so if you have made them ahead of time, steam them again before eating. Delicious served drizzled with maple syrup and a dollop of cream on the side.

coconut layered dessert

serves 6–8

130 g (4¹/2 oz/³/4 cup) **rice flour**

55 g (2 oz/¹/2 cup) **tapioca flour**

170 g (6 oz/³/4 cup) **caster (superfine) sugar**

250 ml (9 fl oz/1 cup) thick **coconut cream** (see tip)

1¹/2 teaspoons **coconut essence**

red food colouring

green food colouring

Combine the rice flour, tapioca flour and sugar in a bowl. In another bowl, mix together the coconut cream, coconut essence and 375 ml (13 fl oz/1 1/2 cups) of cold water. Make a well in the centre of the flour, pour in the liquid and whisk together gently to remove any lumps and make a smooth batter. Strain.

Divide the mixture equally into three portions. Leave one quantity white. Using a few drops of food colouring, tint one of the remaining quantities pale pink and the other pale green. Lightly grease and line the base of a rectangular cake tin measuring 22 x 9 cm (8 1/2 x 3 1/2 inches).

Put the cake tin in a large bamboo steamer and sit the steamer over a wok of simmering water. Pour in about 125 ml (4 fl oz/1/2 cup) of white mixture, put the lid on and steam for 8–10 minutes, or until the mixture sets. Add 125 ml (4 fl oz/1/2 cup) of the pink mixture, and cook for another 5 minutes. Repeat with a layer of green. Continue cooking 125 ml (4 fl oz/1/2 cup) quantities in alternating colours until you reach the final layer (you should have 6 layers altogether). Steam the final layer for 10–15 minutes.

Remove the tin from the steamer and allow the dessert to cool in the tin. When cool, run a knife around the edge of the tin and flip out the dessert onto a plate. Remove the paper from the base and cut into slices with a sharp wet knife. This is best stored at room temperature; it will harden if put in the refrigerator.

tip This dessert sets much better if you use thick coconut cream, so it is important to buy a good-quality brand.

Whisk until you have a
smooth batter.

Once the white layer
has **steamed**, pour on a
pink layer.

sticky rice with mango

serves 4

400 g (14 oz/2 cups) **glutinous rice**

250 ml (9 fl oz/1 cup) **coconut milk**

60 g (2¼ oz/⅓ cup) grated **palm sugar**

4 **makrut (kaffir lime) leaves**, crushed

1 stem **lemon grass**, bruised

2 **mangoes**

2 teaspoons grated **palm sugar**, extra

1 **lime**, quartered

Wash the rice under cold running water until the water runs clear. Put it in a bowl, cover with cold water and leave overnight. Drain.

Line a large bamboo steamer with baking paper, punch with holes and put the rice on top. Sit the steamer over a wok of simmering water and steam, covered, until the rice is soft (this will take 30–60 minutes, depending on the size of your steamer).

Meanwhile, put the coconut milk, palm sugar, lime leaves and lemon grass in a small saucepan and stir over low heat until the sugar has dissolved. Bring to a simmer and cook for 5 minutes, or until thickened.

Transfer the soft rice to a large bowl and pour the coconut mixture over the top, fluffing the rice with a fork as you pour to coat the rice evenly. Do not stir or the rice will become gluggy. Cover and leave for 10 minutes to absorb the liquid, then remove the lemon grass and lime leaves.

Cut the cheeks from the mangoes to give four cheeks. Cut through the mango flesh in a lattice pattern, taking care not to cut through the skin, and push the skin up to expose the flesh. Sprinkle with the extra palm sugar and serve with the sticky rice and a lime wedge.

coconut and ginger puddings with lime syrup

serves 6

lime syrup

115 g (4 oz/1/2 cup) **caster (superfine) sugar**

2 **makrut (kaffir lime) leaves**, crushed

2 tablespoons **lime juice**

125 g (41/2 oz) softened **butter**

115 g (4 oz/1/2 cup) **caster (superfine) sugar**

2 **eggs**

155 g (51/2 oz/11/4 cups) **self-raising flour**

2 teaspoons **ground ginger**

1 tablespoon chopped **glacé ginger**

125 ml (4 fl oz/1/2 cup) **coconut milk**

whipped cream, to serve

To make the syrup, put the sugar and 125 ml (4 fl oz/1/2 cup) of water in a saucepan and stir over low heat until the sugar has dissolved. Add the lime leaves, bring to the boil and cook for 5–6 minutes, or until thick and syrupy. Stir in the lime juice and leave to cool. When cool, remove the lime leaves.

Lightly grease six 125 ml (4 fl oz/1/2 cup) ramekins. Using electric beaters, beat the butter and sugar until light and creamy. Add the eggs one at a time, mixing well after each addition. Fold in the sifted flour, ground ginger and glacé ginger alternately with the coconut milk until combined. Spoon the mixture into the ramekins, smooth the surface, then arrange in a bamboo steamer. Sit the steamer over a wok of simmering water and steam, covered, for 15 minutes, or until cooked when tested with a skewer. Cool for 5 minutes, then run a knife around the puddings and turn out onto serving plates. Drizzle with some syrup and serve with whipped cream.

index

First published in 2005 by Murdoch Books Pty Limited
This edition published in 2010

Murdoch Books Australia
Pier 8/9, 23 Hickson Road, Millers Point, NSW 2000
Phone: +61 (0)2 8220 2000 Fax: +61 (0)2 8220 2558
www.murdochbooks.com.au

Murdoch Books UK Limited
Erico House, 6th Floor North, 93–99 Upper Richmond Road
Putney, London SW15 2TG
Phone: + 44 (0) 20 8785 5995 Fax: + 44 (0) 20 8785 5985
www.murdochbooks.co.uk

Chief Executive: Juliet Rogers
Publishing Director: Kay Scarlett

Publisher: Lynn Lewis
Senior Designer: Heather Menzies
Project Managers: Paul McNally, Rachel Carter
Photographer: Ian Hofstetter, Stuart Scott (cover)
Stylist: Katy Holder, Louise Bickle (cover)
Designer: Tracy Loughlin
Production: Kita George

National Library of Australia Cataloguing-in-Publication Data
Title: Wok it.
ISBN 9781741966411 (pbk.).
Series: It series (Sydney, NSW) Notes: Includes index.
Subjects: Wok cookery. Stir frying. One-dish meals.
Dewey Number: 641.774

PRINTED IN CHINA.

IMPORTANT: Those who might be at risk from the effects of salmonella poisoning (the elderly, pregnant women, young children and those suffering from immune deficiency diseases) should consult their doctor with any concerns about eating raw eggs.